MW00593045

SAULSBURY FIRE RESCUE APPARATUS

1956-2003 PHOTO ARCHIVE

Joel L. Gebet

Iconografix

Photo Archive Series

Iconografix
PO Box 446
Hudson, Wisconsin 54016 USA

© 2003 Joel Gebet

All rights reserved. No part of this work may be reproduced or used in any form by any means... graphic, electronic, or mechanical, including photocopying, recording, taping, or any other information storage and retrieval system... without written permission of the publisher.

The information in this book is true and complete to the best of our knowledge. All recommendations are made without any guarantee on the part of the author or Publisher, who also disclaim any liability incurred in connection with the use of this data or specific details.

We acknowledge that certain words, such as model names and designations, mentioned herein are the property of the trademark holder. We use them for purposes of identification only. This is not an official publication.

Iconografix books are offered at a discount when sold in quantity for promotional use. Businesses or organizations seeking details should write to the Marketing Department, Iconografix, at the above address.

Library of Congress Control Number: 2003103544

ISBN 1-58388-106-9

03 04 05 06 07 08 09 5 4 3 2 1

Printed in China

Cover and book design by Dan Perry

Copyediting by Suzie Helberg

Cover photo- New York City, New York — Purchasing well over 50 pieces of fire apparatus from Saulsbury over the past 20 years, the New York City Fire Department was by far the best customer Saulsbury ever had. Five identical heavy rescue units were delivered to the FDNY in 2002, including one to possibly the world's most famous and well-known fire company, the elite Rescue Company One. Built on 2002 E-One Cyclone II chassis, the rescues' 26-foot bodies were all equipped with 20-kilowatt generators and had special compartments for equipment storage built directly into the cab. Note the "Outstanding" lettering on the front of the cab just below the windshield, a favorite saying of FDNY Rescue One's Captain Terry Hatton, one of the main designers of the new rescue trucks. He was killed in the attack on the World Trade Center on September 11, 2001. *Photo by Joel L. Gebet.*

BOOK PROPOSALS

Iconografix is a publishing company specializing in books for transportation enthusiasts. We publish in a number of different areas, including Automobiles, Auto Racing, Buses, Construction Equipment, Emergency Equipment, Farming Equipment, Railroads & Trucks. The Iconografix imprint is constantly growing and expanding into new subject areas.

Authors, editors, and knowledgeable enthusiasts in the field of transportation history are invited to contact the Editorial Department at Iconografix, Inc., PO Box 446, Hudson, WI 54016.

Dedication

This book is gratefully dedicated to the two most important women in my life, my mother Sandra and my wife Adina. Mom, thank you for recognizing and taking the time to help encourage the interests of a young boy who loved fire engines evolve into an interesting and rewarding hobby. Adina, thank you for the love, encouragement, patience, and understanding that has allowed me to become who I am today.

Acknowledgments

Numerous people contributed to this book, but perhaps none of those contributions were as important as those of Alan Saulsbury and his son Eric. Without their taking the time to gather the delivery photos that grace many of the following pages, this book would not have been possible. Your kindness and patience with me will never be forgotten!

A special thank you also needs to be made to all of the photographers and fire apparatus buffs that, without hesitation, offered their photographic collections and information about them to me. They include: Bruce Anderson, John A. Calderone, Jack DeRosset, Bob Dubbert, Bill Friedrich, David Greenberg, Dan Goyer, Alice Greible, John Greible, Neil Haight, Garry Kadzielawski, Juergen Kiefer, Dennis Maag, Shane MacKichan, Dermot Scales, Tom Shand, John Steger, and Dave Stewardson. Thank you again for all of your help!

Last but not least, thank you to all the firefighters, police officers, hazardous material and rescue squad personnel who graciously took the time to pose their apparatus for my contributors and I to photograph. Your efforts were sincerely appreciated!

Foreword

Every small, independent business starts with an "idea or dream" and is usually pursued by a hard-working and passionate individual. That describes my dad, "Sam" Saulsbury! He had a great personality and sincere love of the fire service.

The Saulsbury fire "tradition" started in 1896 at the Tully Fire Department and continued with Sam's service in both career and volunteer fire departments in central New York State. He designed and built a low center of gravity, "flat side" tanker for his own fire department. Sam's unique safety design and low cost tanker was an instant hit. Saulsbury Fire Equipment was already almost 10 years old when he entered the fire apparatus marketplace in the late-1950s.

Being the son of the fire chief was fun and exciting for a youngster and I was "hooked" on the fire service early in my life. I rode to many fires at an early age and watched from the safety of the Chief's car. In grade school, I joined Dad on late-night trips to fire departments while he was selling the new tanker. As a teenager, I started working in the Saulsbury fire truck plant. The family thought that Oklahoma State University's School of Fire Protection would be a natural choice for an 18-year old, fourth-generation fire fighter, so away I went to OSU. My exposure to my Dad's high standards, work ethic, and his passion for the fire industry certainly helped me reach the top of my class at OSU and start a career as a fire protection engineer for a large insurance company.

In 1968, the Saulsbury family decided an achievable goal would be to build our first plant. At that time, my brother Richard and brother-in-law Dave Carlton joined the Sam-and-Alan team. During the next 20 years, the company grew from about $1 million to $8 million in sales and in 1988, our final state-of-the art new plant was built.

This continued growth and success could not have been accomplished without the great Saulsbury family teamwork and sincere, dedicated employees.

From 1988 to 1998, Saulsbury Fire Apparatus grew to over $40 million per year in sales with apparatus delivered throughout the USA, Canada, and export sales. The Saulsbury family, manufacturing, and sales teams were renowned for high quality and very customized apparatus. From FDNY to LA City FD to Anchorage, Saulsbury Fire Apparatus were the leaders in specialized vehicles of all types. These were truly exciting times in our lives! We had "lots of fun" and worked towards a single goal: BEING THE BEST!

I personally owe a huge debt of gratitude to the thousands of customers, employees, and friends that help build Saulsbury's reputation in the American fire apparatus industry.

After the sale of the company in 1998, Saulsbury Fire Apparatus changed rapidly to mirror operations and apparatus of the new owners (E-One and Federal Signal). By 2003, all of the Saulsbury family and most key managers had left for new careers in other areas of the fire industry. And yet, the memory of the "old Saulsbury team" and family operations still lives on and may be reborn in a "new form" in future years.

The last 55 years of Saulsbury Fire Apparatus have certainly flown by fast. We have so much to be thankful for, especially the pride in the name that will hopefully continue for years to come. The history and pride of Saulsbury has been portrayed positively in this book, and I hope you will enjoy our small part in the US fire service!

Sincerely,
Alan Saulsbury

Preble, New York — Fancher L. "Sam" Saulsbury (second from left) and three other former fire chiefs of the Preble, New York Fire Department stand in front of the first fire truck built by Saulsbury. The Ford squad/utility truck, rebuilt by hand by Saulsbury after it was involved in an accident in 1956, would be the first in a long line of truly custom pieces of fire apparatus built by the Saulsbury family. *Photo courtesy Preble Fire Department*

History of Saulsbury Fire Rescue Apparatus

Fancher L. "Sam" Saulsbury's foray into building fire apparatus happened, quite literally, by accident.

While he did not know it at the time, the series of events that would lead to the construction of his first fire engine would be the start of a long line of fire apparatus built by the Saulsbury family; vehicles whose quality, durability, and innovations would become legendary in the fire apparatus industry.

The Saulsbury name was already well known in the fire fighting circles of central New York State and the family even had some past experience with building fire trucks. Henry Saulsbury, Sam's grandfather, was a member and later chief of the Tully Hose Company, the fire department that he helped organized in 1896 to protect his hometown of Tully, New York. As the town's blacksmith, Henry's experience in building wagons made him the perfect choice to build the newly formed fire department's ladder and hose wagons. In 1900, Henry would open the Saulsbury Garage where he would sell the area's first motorized cars.

With his father Carl also serving Tully as a volunteer firefighter, it was no surprise that Sam Saulsbury would soon become a part of the fire service. In 1940, Sam took a position as a part-time firefighter in the nearby town of Cortland where he was living and working for the Brewer Tichener Company, a local forging shop, as a machinist and welder. In 1948, he began selling Ward LaFrance fire apparatus and fire fighting equipment to area fire departments. In 1952, Saulsbury would move to a new home in the nearby town of Preble and would leave the Cortland Fire Department to join the Preble Fire Department. It was that fateful decision that would change Sam's life in just a few short years.

In 1954, Sam would be elected chief of the Preble Fire Department, a position he would hold for the next 10 years. When his department's Ford utility truck was involved in an accident in 1956, Sam immediately volunteered the skills he had learned in Cortland to help rebuild it. After three months of work in the Preble fire station, Sam brought the truck back to its original condition. Impressed with his abilities, the Preble Fire Department's members would award him a contract to build the department's new water tanker later that same year.

Sam immediately set out to build his department the most "state-of-the-art" vehicle in the region. Built on a 1957 Ford cab over chassis, the tanker was equipped with a 250-gallon-per-minute (gpm) rotary pump and a 1,600-gallon steel tank. After its delivery in 1958, word began to spread around the area's fire departments of Preble's new tanker and its local firefighter builder. It was not long before several departments wanted their own "Saulsburys."

From 1957 until 1959, Sam accepted orders and built a handful of tankers for area fire departments from a Chittenango, New York welding shop that he rented space from. By 1960, with requests for his vehicles increasing, Saulsbury began contracting with the Kurtz Welding shop in nearby Marathon, New York to build his orders. This arrangement would allow Sam to utilize the Kurtz's labor, machinery, and materials, and would last for several years. Sam was soon building numerous tankers, brush trucks, and utility vehicles using the name Saulsbury Fire Equipment Corporation. The company's motto, "Fire Apparatus Built for Firemen by Firemen," was especially appropriate, as nearly all of the workers building Sam's trucks were volunteer firefighters in the towns where they lived.

In 1967, Saulsbury received an order from the small West Corners Fire Department for a large utility truck. This order would become one of the most important in the fledgling company's history.

By the mid-1960s, fire departments across the United States were being called upon by their communities to provide services other than just extinguishing fires. With the ever-increasing popularity of the automobile, so came a dramatic increase in automobile accidents. With their resulting injuries, fluid spills, and fires came a need for the fire service to respond with equipment to remedy these situations. Many fire departments began to make use of generators and floodlights to help improve firefighter safety at nighttime incidents. It would not be long before fire departments were looking for a dedicated vehicle that could carry such specialized equipment and the crew of firefighters needed to operate them. To accomplish this, Saulsbury would build the West Corners unit with an 18-foot walk-in body on a Ford C-700 chassis, the first ever walk-in body built by Saulsbury.

By the early 1970s, a very important innovation had come out of the professional racecar circuit. Hydraulic rescue tools were developed to literally spread apart and cut through the mangled metal that would often result from car accidents at such high speeds; accidents that could potentially kill a driver if they could not be quickly freed and treated for their injuries. Named for its manufacturer, Hurst Performance, Incorporated, the "Hurst Tool" would soon be known by the world famous nickname that is still used today, "The Jaws of Life." The fire service would embrace these hydraulic tools with open arms and soon fire departments large and small were looking to order vehicles that were capable of carrying and operating these life-saving devices. That vehicle, destined to be known as the "heavy rescue truck," had already been produced in varying configurations by a handful of companies including Saulsbury.

With orders now literally pouring in from around central New York State for rescue vehicles, Saulsbury would break ground for a new 40,000 square foot manufacturing facility in Tully, New York in 1972. The company would begin production of all vehicles here, except tankers, in early 1973 and would continue to utilize the Kurtz Welding facility for building tankers until 1976, when operations were consolidated into the new Tully facility. By now, Saulsbury had over 100 employees working at the Tully plant.

From the mid- to late-1970s, Saulsbury's reputation for attention to detail and the extremely high quality vehicles that the company produced resulted in ever-increasing orders. Saulsbury began to get the attention of fire departments in other areas outside of central New York State. As the praise of Saulsbury products spread through the fire service community, so did orders from fire departments in nearby states such as Connecticut, Delaware, Maryland, New Jersey, Pennsylvania, and Virginia. As it is said, "good news travels fast," and it also apparently travels far, as could be seen from orders Saulsbury received from such far away places as Anchorage, Alaska; Santiago, Chili; Bogotá, Colombia; and Caracas, Venezuela!

Sam Saulsbury, the man who had lived the American dream of starting a small company that would grow into a multi-million dollar corporation, would pass away in 1978. His wife, Wilda Saulsbury Carlton would assume the role of president while their younger son Alan would become executive vice president. The Saulsbury's older son, Richard, continued in his role as chief financial officer, a position he had held since 1972.

In 1979, the company would build its first stainless steel rescue body. The unit, a small rescue and light truck with a walk-around, open-style body, was built on a Ford C cab and chassis for Port Washington, New York. Saulsbury would soon start to build the majority of its products using that same 12-gauge type 304L stainless steel; the material that would help bolster the company's reputation for building the most durable vehicles in the industry.

In 1981, Saulsbury received what has probably been its single most important order, a custom built heavy rescue truck for one of the New York City Fire Department's five rescue companies, the FDNY's Rescue Company Two. The truck, a 20-foot walk-in rescue body built on an American LaFrance CTC chassis, would give Saulsbury national exposure for having its product utilized by one of the biggest and busiest fire departments in the world. This order not only began the long-standing relationship between Saulsbury and the FDNY, but would also allow for Saulsbury to build a fleet of specialized vehicles for the New York City Police Department's Emergency Services Bureau. It was the start of another long-standing relationship that continues to the present day.

Another immediate benefit was that over the next several years, other large cities such as Atlanta, Charlotte, Chicago, Cincinnati, Cleveland, Hartford, Houston, Los Angeles, Miami, New Orleans, Philadelphia, Phoenix, St. Louis, and San Diego would begin placing orders with Saulsbury for their own pumpers, rescues, and other specialized vehicles.

Once again, the fire services' role in the United States was changing and expanding. The mid- to late-1980s would see Saulsbury's deliveries increase to almost four times what they were just 10 years earlier — to about 100 vehicles per year. It was around this time that the company would change its name to Saulsbury Fire Apparatus.

Along with dramatic increases in responses to incidents involving hazardous materials, more and more fire departments were forming specialized teams trained in confined space, high angle, and urban search and rescue, and were purchasing equipment that could rectify these situations as well as protect their firefighters. To do so required larger vehicles and in 1985 Saulsbury would build its first custom tandem rear axle rescue truck, a 23-foot body mounted on a 1978 Peterbilt chassis for Warrington, Pennsylvania. The popularity of these large rescue trucks, especially with big cities, was enormous. These trucks had the space to be equipped with almost every conceivable tool and gadget to handle any incident and, to someone not involved in the fire service, could be thought of as large "toolboxes on wheels."

The year 1988 was a turning point for the company. Wilda Saulsbury Carlton would step down as president and her son Alan would become president. To keep up with the company's rapid growth, Saulsbury would move into a new, state-of-the-art production facility in Preble, New York, the town where Sam Saulsbury built his first truck. The facility, at 82,000 square feet, was double the size of the Tully plant and would now employ over 225 skilled craftsmen and workers. The Tully location would remain open but would be utilized as a service center and for rebuilding and refurbishing older units.

That same year, Saulsbury would build perhaps its most revolutionary piece of fire apparatus. It was named the "Five-Star." This pumper incorporated in its design several new concepts, including the first Spartan "Euro-Space" cab, a cab that had no dividing wall between the driver and crew compartments, and two separate rear pump control panels. The prototype was placed in service with Lake St. Louis, Missouri, and while no other "Five-Star" units were built, many of the features of the prototype engine were used in numerous other Saulsbury deliveries.

In the early 1990s, Saulsbury would unveil its "Stealth" Series of pumpers, units designed for maximum operational and service simplicity, along with firefighter safety features. These units were equipped with mid-mounted engines, hydraulic actuated valves, and a new Saulsbury innovation, the "Diagrammatic" pump panel, which displayed a color-coded diagram of the unit showing which discharge each gauge and lever controlled.

Saulsbury would continue to produce approximately 125 vehicles a year through the mid and late 1990s. It was during this time that two more types of vehicles were introduced, the "J Series" and the "Scorpion." The "J Series" consisted of units that were built using bolted, modular stainless steel components that could easily be removed for repair or for new compartment arrangements as compared to the standard welded components. The "Scorpion" was a series of engines with a rear mount pump and pump panels that could be located in either the left rear or right rear compartments or above the back step. The company would also change its name for the last time to Saulsbury Fire Rescue.

In 1998, the company would become a wholly owned subsidiary of the Federal Signal Corporation. Alan Saulsbury and his son Eric would continue running the day-to-day operations of the company, but now with the backing and resources of a large publicly held company. Saulsbury was now part of Federal Signal's "Fire-Rescue Group," which included such companies as E-One, Bronto Skylift, and Superior. This arrangement would see Saulsbury now building many vehicles on custom E-One chassis, a chassis never utilized by the company up until that point.

With the new millennium came an even greater increase in Saulsbury's deliveries to fire departments around the world. In 2001, Saulsbury would close its Tully service center and consolidate operations to its Preble plant. In December 2002, Federal Signal announced that Alan Saulsbury—who had been working in a consulting position at Saulsbury since the company's purchase in 1998—would no longer be working for the company his father founded. This left Alan's son Eric Saulsbury as the only Saulsbury family member working at the company. Eric would also leave his position as Saulsbury's sales manager in early 2003 and in May of that same year, Federal Signal, inexplicably removed the Saulsbury name from the Preble plant. Time will only tell if the move was to enable Federal Signal to build "Saulsburys" from their other fire apparatus manufacturing plants in Florida and Canada or if the name will just be permanently deleted from its "Fire-Rescue" group.

Over the course of its 47 years in building fire and rescue apparatus, Saulsbury produced over 3,000 custom vehicles that served both municipal and non-municipal fire departments, rescue squads, and police departments on four continents. Its motto of "quality people making quality products" speaks volumes for one of the finest fire apparatus builders the fire service community has ever known.

Preble, New York — The first order Sam Saulsbury received for his own custom-built piece of fire apparatus was from his own fire department, Preble, in 1957. Sam set out to build them the most advanced tanker at the time and when he was finished in 1958, the unit was just that. Built on a Ford C chassis, the low center-of-gravity "flatside" tanker was equipped with a 250-gpm rotary pump, a 1,600-gallon steel water tank, and a top-mounted booster hose reel. Originally painted red, the tanker was repainted white to match the department's other vehicles sometime during the 1970s. *Photo by the late Jack B. Greible*

Owasco, New York — One of the first tankers built by Saulsbury was this sharp-looking, all-white Ford 700 conventional job. This small-town fire engine was well equipped with a 350-gpm pump, 1,600-gallon steel water tank, a booster line, and overhead ladder rack. Note the compartment in front of the pump panel and the siren on the front fender. *Photo courtesy Saulsbury Fire Rescue*

Shelton, Connecticut — An example of the style of tanker that was very popular with Saulsbury's first customers was this 1966 unit built on a Ford C-850 chassis. Truck 9 was equipped with a 350-gpm pump and a 1,500-gallon water tank. Note the row of eight "Indian Tanks" used for brush fires and the Federal "Q" mechanical siren mounted just below the front windshield. *Photo courtesy Saulsbury Fire Rescue*

West Corners Fire Company, Endicott, New York — This nifty little red and white squad truck would turn out to be the first Saulsbury vehicle built with a walk-in body; the precursor to the heavy rescue vehicle that would become so popular in just a few short years. Built on a 1967 Ford C-700 chassis, Squad 34's 18-foot body had four compartments and two large spotlights on each side. Note the siren speaker mounted just below the front windshield. *Photo courtesy West Corners Fire Company*

SAULSBURY
FIRE EQUIPMENT CO.
—TULLY, NEW YORK—

—CUSTOM-BUILT—
PUMPER-TANKERS, TANKERS, BRUSH TRUCKS, AND RESCUE APPARATUS

"FIRE APPARATUS BUILT FOR FIREMEN BY FIREMEN"

This Saulsbury brochure from the late 1960s showed a company that was well on its way to success. The tanker pictured, still at that time the company's most popular product, was delivered to White Springs, New York in 1966. Note the company's new slogan of "Fire Apparatus Built for Firemen by Firemen." *Photo courtesy Saulsbury Fire Rescue*

Port Jervis, New York — The Fowler Rescue and Salvage Company Number Three had the distinction of owning one of the most unusual and impressive heavy rescues ever built by Saulsbury. This 1972 Ward LaFrance Ambassador Series, the only chassis of its type built with a heavy rescue body, was equipped with a 250-gpm pump, 300-gallon water tank, 12-kilowatt generator, and 30,000-pound hydraulic winch. The rescue's flowing rear bodywork lines and its all-white paint job combined for a truly magnificent appearance. It is interesting to note the dramatic improvement in design that took place in the six years since the first Saulsbury walk-in body was built. *Photo by Jack DeRosset*

Trainer, Pennsylvania — While Saulsbury's first years were originally known for their custom tankers, the company also built a large number of smaller mini-pumpers and brush fire trucks, as well. A good example of that type of Saulsbury product was this white over light blue 1974 Dodge Power Wagon. This little four-wheel-drive rig packed quite a punch with its 275-gpm PTO pump, 250-gallon water tank, and assortment of onboard equipment that included two floodlights and a Stokes basket. Note the small booster hose on the front bumper of the truck that allowed a firefighter to spray water on a fire while the engine was moving. *Photo by Joel L. Gebet*

Fuller Road Fire Department, Colonie, New York — The heavy rescue truck was becoming increasingly more popular in 1975 when this unit was delivered to this town just outside of Albany. A state-of-the-art vehicle for its time, the rescue's 21-foot body, built on a Ford C chassis, had such features as a 7-kilowatt PTO generator, a floodlight system that could be controlled from the cab, and a custom Formica finish inside the body and compartments. *Photo courtesy Saulsbury Fire Rescue*

McLean, New York — Very few pieces of fire apparatus were built using Brockway "Huskie" chassis, and this was one of only two built with Saulsbury bodywork. Delivered in 1975, this basic water tanker was equipped with only an 1,800-gallon tank and a specially designed "locker" compartment located just behind the cab. Note the exhaust stack between the cab and body and the ladders mounted above the tank. *Photo courtesy Saulsbury Fire Rescue*

Islip, New York — City service ladder trucks, units that carried a full compliment of ground ladders but did not have a hydraulically-operated ladder, were rare finds by the 1970s. Saulsbury delivered this unique truck to this fire department on New York's Long Island in 1976. It had bench seating in the middle of the open body and carried over 140 feet of ladders and ladder company tools. Note the Federal "Q" mechanical siren underneath the front bumper. *Photo by Joel L. Gebet*

Ansonia, Connecticut — This unusual 18-foot open body squad unit was built by Saulsbury on a 1977 Pemfab chassis for this small city fire department located north of New Haven. With its high-pressure 1,200-psi PTO pump, 300-gallon water tank, eight bottle air cascade system, and six-kilowatt generator, Squad Attack Nine was well-suited to handle almost any incident that this fire department might face all on its own. This unit had an enormous amount of compartment space including three compartments built into the front of the body behind the jump seat area. *Photo by Joel L. Gebet*

Syracuse, New York — Saulsbury delivered this imposing chrome yellow rescue truck to the Syracuse Fire Department's Rescue Company One in 1977. Built on an International Paystar 5000 chassis with access to the 18-foot body from the cab, it was the first such "walk-through" truck built by Saulsbury. Its list of features, impressive for the time, included a 17-kilowatt generator, an 8,000-pound A-Frame crane and a 20,000-pound winch in the extended front bumper, and perhaps most important, four-wheel drive for the rough central New York State winters. Note the warning lights mounted on the front fender and the top of the grille. *Photo by Tom Shand*

East Fishkill, New York — The Saulsbury "Seneca" series of tanker units was the perfect all-purpose fire engine for small town fire departments. Built on a 1978 Ford F-700 chassis, Tank 4 had a 400-gpm pump, a 1,250-gallon water tank with a six-inch rear quick-dump valve, an enclosed booster reel, four storage compartments, and an overhead ladder rack. *Photo courtesy Saulsbury Fire Rescue*

Envirogas Incorporated, Mayville, New York — Saulsbury delivered very few units to industrial fire departments. This interesting little dry chemical unit, painted using the company's colors of red and black, was utilized by Envirogas to protect its numerous natural gas wells throughout western New York State. Built on a 1980 Chevrolet Scottsdale 30 4x4 chassis, it was equipped with a "Fire Boss" dry chemical system and carried 500 pounds of Purple K and 500 pounds of dry chemical extinguishing agents. *Photo courtesy Saulsbury Fire Rescue*

Cuyler, New York — Another example of a well-equipped Saulsbury mini-pumper was this unit that was originally built to help protect the venues of the 1980 Winter Olympics in Lake Placid, New York. When the games were completed, the Cuyler Fire Department purchased the 750-gpm engine that was built on a four-wheel-drive Chevrolet K-30 chassis. *Photo courtesy Saulsbury Fire Rescue*

Port Washington, New York — While this little squad truck may not be the most impressive piece of apparatus Saulsbury built, it was definitely one of the most important. Delivered in 1980, it was the first Saulsbury-built body made from the type 304L stainless steel it would become so famous for. The open rescue body was equipped with bench seating and had three floodlights, two spotlights, and ladders mounted on each side of the unit. *Photo by Joel L. Gebet*

New York City, New York — Another important Saulsbury vehicle was delivered to the world's biggest fire department, the FDNY, in 1982. Built on the rare American LaFrance CTC chassis, this 20-foot heavy rescue truck was the first Saulsbury delivery to the FDNY and would pave the way for Saulsbury to receive international exposure for its products. The unit was assigned to Rescue Company Number Two that covers the borough of Brooklyn. Note Rescue 2's company "logo" on the driver's door featuring an angry bulldog wearing a fire helmet. *Photo courtesy Saulsbury Fire Rescue*

New York City, New York — Even though the world-famous FDNY Superpumper System was placed out of service in 1982, the department decided to keep in service the six Satellite hose wagons that were part of that system. The next Saulsbury deliveries to the FDNY would be four brand new Satellite units for the newly created "Maxi-Water System." Built on 1982 American LaFrance Century chassis, the units' main features were their massive Stang deluge guns capable of flowing 4,000 gallons of water per minute! *Photo courtesy Saulsbury Fire Rescue*

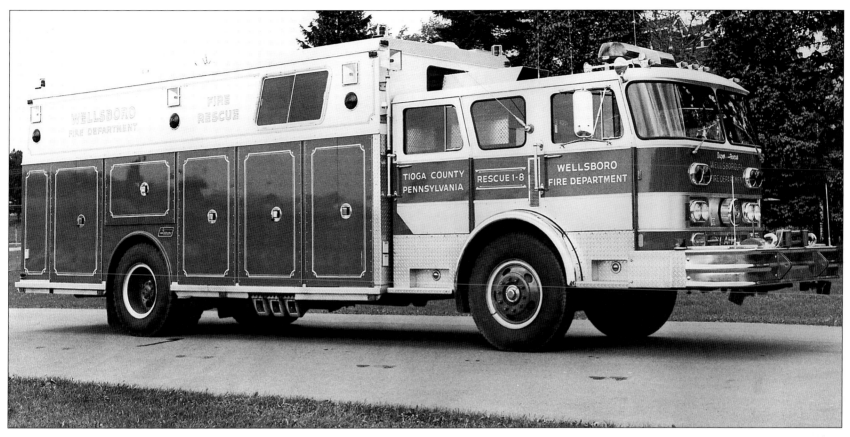

Wellsboro, Pennsylvania — Located in the rural north-central part of the state, this small-town fire department had a rescue truck that would be the envy of their big-city counterparts. When it was delivered in 1982, Rescue 1-8, built on a Hahn chassis and equipped with a 300-gpm PTO pump and a 200-gallon water tank, was one of the biggest and best equipped heavy rescue trucks in the United States. Note the roof-mounted strobe lights on the corners of the walk-in rescue body and the early use of an air conditioner on the cab roof. *Photo courtesy Saulsbury Fire Rescue*

Rescue 1-8's pump panel, generator, numerous Hannay cable reels, and large amount of exterior compartment space. Note the three quartz lights recessed into the rescue body. *Photo courtesy Saulsbury Fire Rescue*

Bethesda, Maryland — The Bethesda Chevy Chase Rescue Squad operated this unusual 1982 Kenworth K100 with a 21-foot Saulsbury body, a very rare chassis for emergency vehicles. It was equipped with two separate generators, a 15-kilowatt hydraulic and a six-kilowatt diesel, as well as a Will-Burt light tower and a 30,000-pound winch. This rig was painted white with gold stripes. Note the three "Mars" lights just below the windshield. *Photo courtesy Saulsbury Fire Rescue*

Philadelphia, Pennsylvania — The Philadelphia Fire Department operated two of these 1982 Ford C tandem axle chemical units, the first Saulsbury vehicles built with roll-up doors. Chemical 1, manned by the firefighters of Engine Company 60 in the South Philadelphia section of the city, carried 1,000 pounds of Purple K, 1,000 gallons of alcohol foam, a 1,500-cubic-feet-per-minute (cfm) air cascade system, and tools and equipment to support the department's hazardous materials team. Note the small pump panel and the large dry chemical tank behind the cab. *Photo by Joel L. Gebet*

Diamond Fire Company, Walnutport, Pennsylvania — Not only did Saulsbury build their own trucks, but from 1976 until 1984 the company and its distributors sold American LaFrance fire apparatus as well. This arrangement allowed Saulsbury to build several of their bodies on American LaFrance chassis, including this massive all-white "Mohawk" series tanker delivered to this fire company located in the northeastern part of the state near Allentown. Delivered in 1982, Tanker 2921 had a 450-gpm pump and a 3,200-gallon water tank. Note the Mars light mounted in the front of the cab. *Photo by Joel L. Gebet*

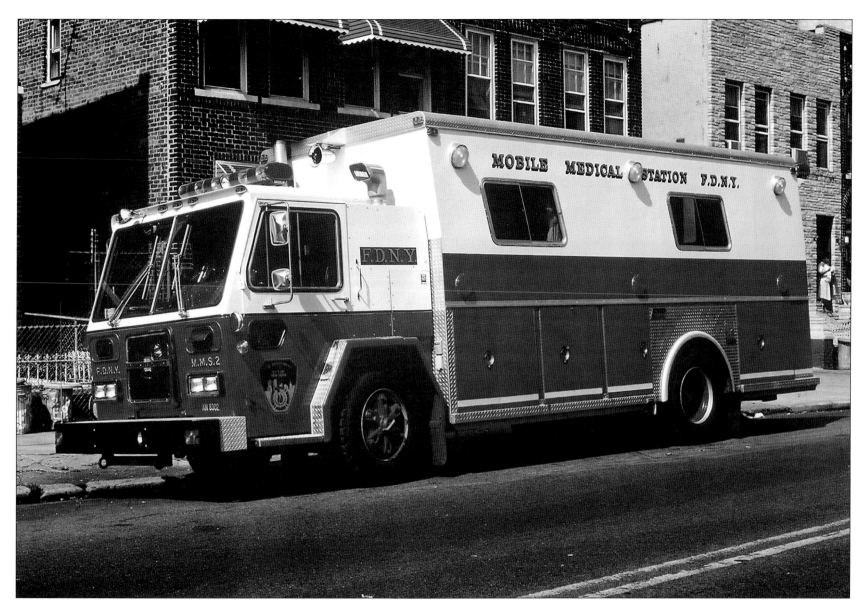

New York City, New York — Looking very much like the heavy rescue truck delivered to the FDNY's Rescue 2 the previous year is this 1983 unit that served a much different purpose. Assigned as Mobile Medical Station 2, this unit, one of two delivered by Saulsbury, functioned as a small emergency room at multiple alarm fires and provided immediate and advanced medical care to firefighters injured at these incidents. Note the siren speaker mounted on the body just above the cab's roof. *Photo by John A. Calderone*

Emmaus, Pennsylvania — This interesting unit was the first Saulsbury heavy rescue truck built with roll-up doors. Delivered in 1984, it was built on a Hahn chassis with an 84-inch cab and a 16-foot aluminum body. Among its numerous features were a 15-kilowatt generator, two 3,600-psi air cylinders for operating air tools, and four 1,500-watt quartz lights on all four corners of the body. Note the jump seat mounted on the rescue body just behind the cab and the four compartments above the roll-up doors. *Photo courtesy Saulsbury Fire Rescue*

Breezy Point, Queens, New York — Few people are aware that the United States' largest city still has 10 volunteer fire departments protecting life and property. All of these departments were organized to protect the outlying areas of the city before the FDNY opened fire stations nearby. One of the five operating in the borough of Queens is the Point Breeze Fire Department, located on the western tip of the Far Rockaway peninsula. With their response area covering a community with the majority of its roads being nothing more than sand, the department ordered this small and very unusual International S1800 in 1984 equipped with four-wheel drive and Saulsbury bodywork. Nicknamed the "Sand Flea," Engine Seven had a 1,000-gpm front-mount pump and carried 375 gallons of water. Note that the engine has only a single rear tire for off-road driving on sand. *Photo by Joel L. Gebet*

IBM Corporation, Endicott, New York — Looking very much like a heavy rescue truck, this rather plain-looking unit was actually designed to be used as a pumper at the world-renowned computer-maker IBM's Endicott plant. The facility's Emergency Control Brigade received the unusual vehicle, another of the relatively rare Saulsbury industrial deliveries, painted all white and equipped with a 750-gpm pump, 300-gallon water tank, and 20-gallon foam tank, in 1985. *Photo by Tom Shand*

Paramus, New Jersey — This unusual foam unit was built on a 1985 Ford C-8000 chassis for the Paramus Fire Department's Company Three, which was responsible for operating the department's hazardous materials units. The short-wheelbase engine had a 1,000-gpm pump, 400-gallon foam tank, and a 750-pound Purple K dry chemical system. Note the two rows of foam cans on the side of the engine's body and the deck gun designed specifically for foam operations. *Photo by Joel L. Gebet*

Warrington, Pennsylvania — This rescue unit has quite a story behind it. Delivered in 1985, it would be the first tandem rear axle heavy rescue truck built by Saulsbury. The truck chassis, a 1978 Peterbuilt, was originally purchased by the Port Authority of New York and New Jersey and was used as an armored car until 1984. Firefighters from the Warrington Fire Department bought the truck from a junkyard, removed the original armored car body and completely rebuilt the chassis. The Peterbuilt chassis was then turned over to Saulsbury who completely rebuilt the cab and added a new 23-foot walk-in rescue box equipped with two separate 12-kilowatt generators and a 20,000-pound winch. *Photo courtesy Saulsbury Fire Rescue*

A view of the right side of the rescue showing the side entrance to the body. The two "boxes" visible just under the front windshield are twin 500-watt spotlights. *Photo by Joel L. Gebet*

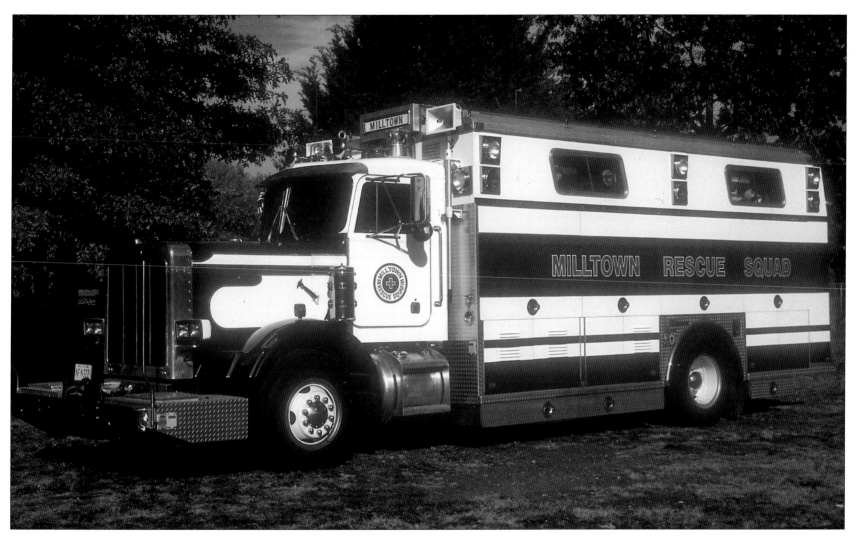

Milltown, New Jersey — This large heavy rescue truck (the first Saulsbury body to be built on a Peterbilt conventional chassis) was delivered to this small-town rescue squad that is responsible for protecting a portion of the very busy New Jersey Turnpike. The body, built in 1985, was mounted on the 1984 Peterbilt 359 chassis and was equipped with a 20-kilowatt generator, a 40-cfm air compressor, and two winches; a 22,000-pound front-mounted unit and a 12,000-pound rear-mounted unit. This impressive unit is painted white with dark metallic green stripes. Note that the small "Milltown" lettering on the top of the rescue body just above the cab is actually a backlit sign that is visible at night, a unique feature that is present on all of the rescue squad's vehicles. *Photo by Joel L. Gebet*

Swedesburg, Pennsylvania — This unique Saulsbury rescue pumper was delivered to this small town located outside Philadelphia in 1985. The Hahn "92" cab and chassis selected for Rescue 8-1 would become one of the most popular custom chassis chosen by Saulsbury customers during the mid- to late-1980s. The rescue's impressive list of features included a 400-gpm PTO pump with three crosslays, 500-gallon water tank, 20-kilowatt generator, Will-Burt 7,000-watt light tower and a 12-bottle air cascade system. The pump panel was located in the first compartment behind the cab. *Photo by Joel L. Gebet*

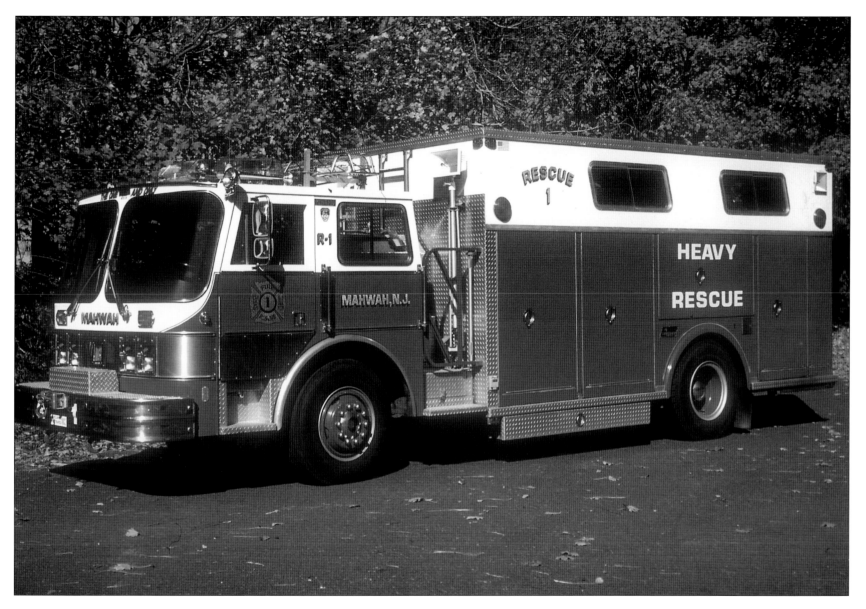

Mahwah, New Jersey — Another Saulsbury sporting the then newly released Hahn "92" cab and chassis was the Mahwah Fire Department's Rescue One. Delivered in 1986, the walk-in unit, made even more interesting with its open canopy cab, was equipped with a 25-kilowatt generator and front-mounted winch. Note the Stokes rescue basket mounted on the cab roof over the jump seat area and the winch mounted inside the diamond plate box on the front bumper. *Photo by Joel L. Gebet*

Syracuse, New York — The second Saulsbury-built heavy rescue truck delivered to the Syracuse Fire Department was this massive 1986 International Paystar 5070 chassis. Rescue One had a 24-foot body that could be accessed from the cab and was equipped with a 17-kilowatt PTO generator and a 20,000-pound front-mounted hydraulic winch. Note the warning light mounted on the front fender that is similar to the previous 1977 rescue. *Photo by Tom Shand*

Seaford, Delaware — The only Saulsbury vehicle ever built utilizing a Pierce Manufacturing chassis was delivered to this small town fire department located in the southwestern part of the state near the Maryland border in 1986. Heavy Rescue 87-6's 22-foot walk-in Saulsubury body was mounted on a Pierce Arrow cab and chassis and it was equipped with a 20-kilowatt generator, a six bottle air cascade system, and a 12,000-watt light tower. *Photo courtesy Saulsbury Fire Rescue*

Seaford, New York — New quadruple combination fire apparatus (known as quads because they were equipped with a pump, water tank, hose, and a full compliment of ground ladders) were very rare finds in the 1980s. One of those rare trucks, a Saulsbury-built quad, was delivered to this Long Island fire department in 1986. The long wheelbase unit, built on a custom American LaFrance Century chassis, had a 1,500-gpm pump and a 600-gallon water tank. *Photo by Joel L. Gebet*

Clinton, New Jersey — Due to the fact that their station's bay door had a very low overhead clearance, the Clinton First Aid and Rescue Squad chose Saulsbury to build them this unusually low-profile heavy rescue truck with a walk-in body. Built on a 1986 Ford C chassis, this compact 18-foot rescue truck packed a lot of punch in its 18-foot body with its 12-kilowatt generator, 12,000-pound front winch, and eight-bottle 5,000-psi air cascade system. Rescue 45-56 was painted in an interesting white and red color scheme. *Photo by Joel L. Gebet*

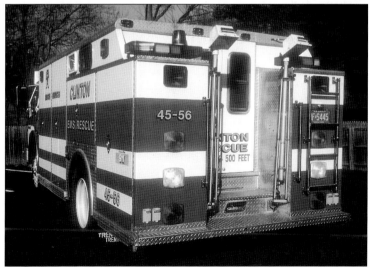

A view of the rear of this rescue shows its very low height walk-in body. *Photo by Joel L. Gebet*

New York City, New York — The FDNY's Field Communications Unit (known locally as the Field Comm), utilized at multiple alarm fires as a command post and equipped with numerous radios, cellular phones and other communications equipment, received this Mack R walk-in unit from Saulsbury in 1987. *Photo by John A. Calderone*

A rear view of the Field Comm shows the door to the unit's body as well as its two air conditioning units mounted behind the diamond plate boxes on the rear of the truck. *Photo courtesy Saulsbury Fire Rescue*

Odessa, Delaware — This small coastal town received this very large heavy rescue truck from Saulsbury in 1987. Salvage Rescue Unit 24-6 was equipped with a 300-gpm PTO pump and a 200-gallon water tank. The large diamond plate box on the front bumper contains a large reel for hydraulic rescue tool operations. Note the mural on the top rear of the rescue body of the cartoon character *Bluto* carrying a Hurst Tool. *Photo by Joel L. Gebet*

Syracuse, New York — The first Saulsbury vehicles built with aerials was an order of three Spartan Monarch four-wheel drive chassis equipped with LTI 55-foot "Fire Stix" booms in 1987. The engines also had 2,000-gpm pumps and 500-gallon water tanks and were painted chrome yellow. Note the light bar mounted on the cab below the front windshield. *Photo courtesy Saulsbury Fire Rescue*

A view of the officer's side of the truck showing the crane in its stowed position and the entrance to the walk-in body. *Photo by Joel L. Gebet*

Livingston, New Jersey — Another 1987 company first for Saulsbury was the first rescue truck built with a crane that was delivered to this northern New Jersey town. Built on a Mack MC Fire Chassis, the unit's 19-foot body was equipped with a rear-mounted, 25-foot hydraulic National Crane with a 10,000-pound lift capacity and a 15-kilowatt hydraulic generator. *Photo courtesy Saulsbury Fire Rescue*

Lake St. Louis, Missouri — One of the most innovative and radically designed vehicles ever built by Saulsbury was an engine named the "Five Star." A 1988 joint venture between Saulsbury and Spartan Motors, the unit was the first to be built on Spartan's new "Euro-Space" chassis, which did not have a wall between the driver and crew compartments found on all fire apparatus cabs of the period. Complete with two separate pump panels, the main one was an all-electric "Diagrammatic" unit designed by Fire Research Corporation of Nesconset, New York, and was the first such pump panel ever built. Top-mounted at the left rear of the engine, the panel, which moved the operator away from the noise and danger of the street and gave him an unobstructed view of the incident scene, controlled the engine's 1,500-gpm pump and onboard 750-gallon water and 100-gallon foam tanks. The cab had unique styling such as headlights mounted in the front bumper and a bright lime green paint job with dark green stripes. *Photo by Dennis J. Maag*

Lake St. Louis, Missouri — A rear view of the Five Star engine shows the engine's secondary pump panel, and its intakes and discharges. The two compartments behind the engine's brake lights and turn signals each contained two modules of 150 feet of 1 3/4-inch hose. Many of the engine's design features were common in European fire apparatus but almost totally new for the American fire apparatus industry and, unfortunately due in part to that culture shock, the prototype purchased by the Lake St. Louis Fire Protection District was the only one ever built. *Photo courtesy Saulsbury Fire Rescue*

Setauket, New York — The Setauket Fire Department had the distinction of operating the first Saulsbury engine built with a pump panel located inside the crew cab. The panel was also the second "Diagrammatic" pump panel produced by Fire Research for Saulsbury to use in one of their vehicles. The engine, built on a 1988 Spartan chassis painted white over chrome yellow, was equipped with a 1,500-gpm pump and carried 750 gallons of water, and 100 gallons of foam. Note the booster reel, Federal "Q" mechanical siren, and the two air horns, all mounted on the front bumper. *Photo courtesy Saulsbury Fire Rescue*

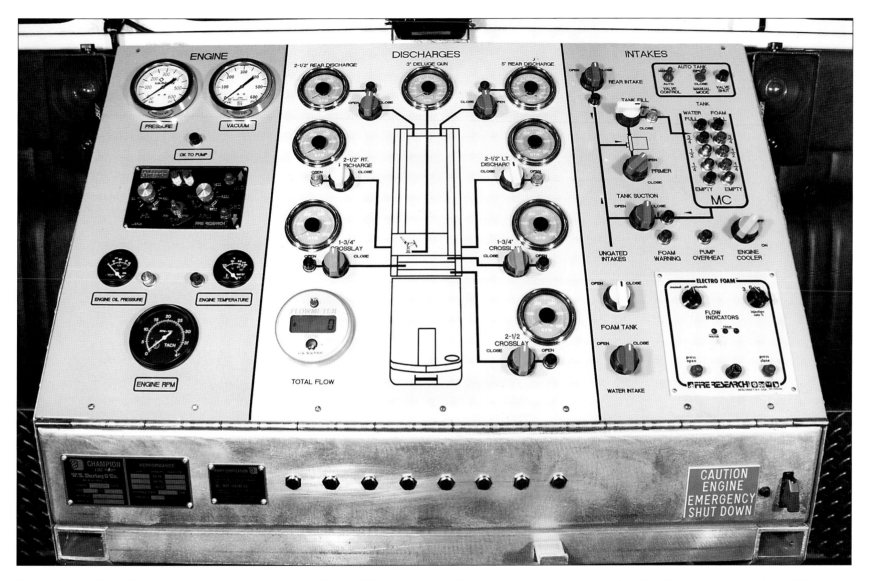

Setauket, New York — A close-up view of the "Diagrammatic" pump panel used in the Setauket engine. The all-electric panel, designed and built by Fire Research of Nesconset, New York, is laid out for the pump's operator in three sections. The left section shows the engine conditions such as rpm, oil pressure and temperature, as well as the controls for the pump's pressure governor. The middle section is the actual "diagrammatic" portion with a color-coded outline of the engine showing the type and gpm of each discharge. The right and final section is for use and control of the engine's onboard water and foam tanks and foam system. *Photo courtesy Saulsbury Fire Rescue*

New York City, New York — The FDNY received five of these massive Saulsbury-built heavy rescues between 1985 and 1989. Rescue Companies Three and Four's trucks were built in 1988 with 25-foot rescue bodies and were equipped with 15-kilowatt generators, rear-mounted winches, and 30-foot telescoping light towers mounted directly behind the cab. Each of the five units had large amounts of eye-catching graphics on the bodies including large murals of the individual companies' logos. Rescue Three's logo was "Big Blue." *Photo by Dermot Scales*

South Fire District, Middletown, Connecticut — The first American LaFrance chassis to be produced after the company re-emerged from bankruptcy in 1986 was known as the "Century 2000." The South Fire District has the distinction of owning the only Century 2000 Series chassis to receive Saulsbury bodywork. Tanker 30, delivered in 1988, had a 1,500-gpm pump and carried 2,000 gallons of water. *Photo by Joel L. Gebet*

Bellmawr, New Jersey — This large rescue pumper was delivered to this southern New Jersey fire department in 1988. Built on a Spartan Gladiator chassis, Rescue Pumper 325 had a 1,500-gpm pump and carried 750 gallons of water, 100 gallons of foam, and a 15-kilowatt generator. The unit was painted all white with a blue stripe. Note the foam deluge gun mounted just above the pump panel. *Photo courtesy Saulsbury Fire Rescue*

Greenville, New York — Perhaps one of the most unusual deliveries ever made by Saulsbury was to this small town located south west of Albany in 1988. Built on a massive GMC General conventional chassis, the truck has the outward appearance of a large pumper-tanker. A walk to the rear of the vehicle shows that it is actually an 18-foot walk-in rescue body! Painted white with a large red stripe, the unit had a 1,500-gpm pump, a 500-gallon water tank, a 12-kilowatt generator, and an onboard air cascade system. *Photo by Joel L. Gebet*

A rear view of the Greenville rescue-pumper's unusual walk-in body. *Photo by Joel L. Gebet*

Middlesex County, New Jersey — Located just southwest of New York City, this heavily industrialized county's busy hazardous materials unit placed this massive Saulsbury-built tandem axle unit in service in 1989. Built on a Mack MC chassis, HM-5 was one of the biggest and best equipped vehicles of its type in the country and included such features as a 250-gpm PTO pump, a 175-gallon water tank, a six-bottle air cascade system, dual weather stations, a communications console, an onboard 55-gallon drum storage area with hoist, and even a sink with hot and cold running water. It is painted in a striking white over dark metallic blue paint scheme with white and yellow stripes. *Photo by Joel L. Gebet*

Vorhees, New Jersey — The Kresson Fire District operated this interesting 1989 Mack R heavy rescue. A tour of Rescue 6636 would have revealed equipment such as a 300-gpm pump, a 300-gallon water tank, a 25-kilowatt generator, a four-bottle air cascade system, and a 12,000-pound winch. Note the four square headlights on the front of the cab, an interesting departure from the two circular headlights found on almost all Mack R cabs. *Photo courtesy Saulsbury Fire Rescue*

Coram, New York — During the late-1980s, Saulsbury entered into an agreement with Baker to build the bodies for their Aerialscope tower ladders built on Mack CF chassis. The first to be delivered to this department located on New York's Long Island was also the only quint of this type that Saulsbury built, a 1989 unit equipped with a 1,500-gpm pump, a 250-gallon water tank, and a 75-foot boom. *Photo by Tom Shand*

New York City, New York — The FDNY placed an order with Saulsbury for two of these Tactical Support Units in 1989. Not only did they replace the FDNY's two aging floodlight trucks but they also gave the department vehicles that could be used at numerous types of emergency incidents in addition to being used for nighttime lighting. The results were these two 1990 Ford F Super Duty units with Reading bodies heavily modified by Saulsbury to include a 15-kilowatt generator, a 30-foot, 9,000-watt light tower, and a Zodiac inflatable 14-foot boat that was mounted on the top of the unit. *Photo courtesy Saulsbury Fire Rescue*

Saulsbury goes Hollywood! This highly unusual looking truck, built on a 1964 GMC/H and H rescue truck that formerly had served Union City, New Jersey, and later Mahwah, New Jersey, was designed for the National Broadcasting Company's police drama "True Blue," a fictional account of the everyday lives of officers assigned to the New York City Police Department's Emergency Services Bureau. The truck was completely rebuilt from its original configuration in 1989 to include such "features" as a hydraulic crane, roof-mounted gun turret, four stabilizer jacks, telescoping pole with lights and television camera, and a retractable bullet-proof front windshield, none of which actually functioned and none of which could be found on real NYPD Emergency Services Bureau trucks. Saulsbury craftsmen completed the project in an unbelievable three weeks and while the television show lasted for only one season, the truck still makes an occasional appearance in other NBC police shows set in New York City. *Photo by the late Jack B. Greible*

Elmont, New York — While the Mack CF was one of the most popular and recognizable fire apparatus chassis, only a handful were ever built with raised-roof cabs. To get a Mack CF with a raised roof required major modification by the company building the apparatus body, as Mack did not manufacture them this way. Saulsbury built only two vehicles with customized Mack CF raised-roof cabs, one of which was this 1989 heavy rescue with a 22-foot body for this Nassau County department located on the eastern border with New York City's borough of Queens. *Photo by Joel L. Gebet*

Plymouth, Massachusetts — Very few pieces of fire apparatus were built using the extremely heavy-duty Mack RM conventional chassis. Possibly the biggest tanker that Saulsbury ever built was this brute for the Plymouth Fire Department's Tanker One. Delivered in 1989, the massive unit was equipped with a 500-gpm pump, 2,500-gallon water tank, and three crosslays and was painted a striking red with black fenders and compartments. *Photo by Joel L. Gebet*

New York City, New York — Impressed with the quality of Saulsbury's deliveries to the FDNY, the New York City Police Department placed several orders of its own with Saulsbury in the late-1980s and early 1990s for new heavy-duty rescue-type vehicles for its 10 Emergency Service Units (ESU). Truck 4, located in the Kingsbridge section of the Bronx, received this white over light blue unit, one of two delivered that were built on a Mack DM chassis, in 1990. The trucks, while equipped with hydraulic rescue tools, SCUBA and dive rescue equipment, SCBAs and spare bottles, hazardous materials and decontamination equipment and medical supplies, were primarily built to transport the ESU's arsenal of SWAT weaponry. *Photo by Joel L. Gebet*

Chicago, Illinois — The first Saulsbury delivery to the "Windy City" was this 1990 Spartan Gladiator with a three-door cab and a 21-foot walk-in body that was custom designed and built for the fire department's Hazardous Incident Team. Features included a command area complete with a computer terminal, cellular phones, and fax machine in the rear of the cab, and a special stainless steel interior laboratory equipped with a hydrocarbon testing fume enclosure with an explosion-proof exhaust fan. *Photo courtesy Saulsbury Fire Rescue*

St. Louis, Missouri — St. Louis is another major city that received their first Saulsbury vehicles in 1990; two of these monstrous tandem axle rescues were built on Spartan Gladiator chassis and were assigned to the city's two rescue companies. The 21-foot walk-in rescue bodies were equipped with extensive roof compartments, a 125-cfm air compressor with two electric air cable reels, a 20-kilowatt generator, and front and rear 12,000-pound winches. Note the "Arrowstick" traffic directional light bar mounted on the roof in the middle of the rescue body. *Photo by Dennis J. Maag*

Anaheim, California — This Spartan squad is one of two vehicles Saulsbury delivered in 1990 to this Southern California city known as the home of Disneyland. Built on a Spartan "Silent Knight" chassis with a rear-mounted engine, the unit was well equipped with such features as a hydraulic ladder rack, a four-bottle 5,000-psi air cascade system, a Will-Burt 9,000-watt light tower, and a 12,000-pound electric winch. *Photo by the late Jack B. Greible*

A view of the rear of the truck shows the ladder rack deployed and the rear-mounted engine and the built-in stairs around the engine housing designed to access the compartments on top of the rescue body. *Photo by the late Jack B. Greible*

Jericho, New York — The only other Mack CF chassis to receive a Saulsbury custom-built raised roof cab was this very interesting all-white engine delivered in 1991 to this department located on Long Island. Built on an already-extended cab, Engine 943 was equipped with a 1,500-gpm pump, a 500-gallon water tank, and a 50-gallon foam tank. Note the mural of Trident Engine Company Three's logo of Neptune on the crew cab door. *Photo by Joel L. Gebet*

New York City, New York — Unfortunately, all good things must come to an end. The Mack CF chassis with a Baker Aerialscope elevating platform was one of the most popular and recognizable pieces of fire apparatus ever built, in large measure because of its extensive use by the FDNY. The last of this type of truck to be built, a 1991 Mack CF with Saulsbury bodywork equipped with a 95-foot Aerialscope platform, was delivered to the FDNY in 1992 and assigned to Ladder 58 in the Bronx, where it remained in service until early 2003. It was also the last piece of fire apparatus built on a Mack CF chassis to be operated by the FDNY. *Photo by John A. Calderone*

Anchorage, Alaska — The proven reliability of Saulsbury's products in the brutally cold New York State winters was a major selling point for the Anchorage Fire Department, who purchased three of these 2,500-gallon tandem axle water tankers from Saulsbury in 1992. Built on Freightliner FLC conventional chassis with three driving axles, the tankers' firefighting capabilities were provided by 750-gpm PTO pumps. Saulsbury designed the tankers' hose beds to carry 800 feet of three-inch hose, a folding water tank, 59 feet of ground ladders, and three lengths of hard suction hose. *Photo courtesy Saulsbury Fire Rescue*

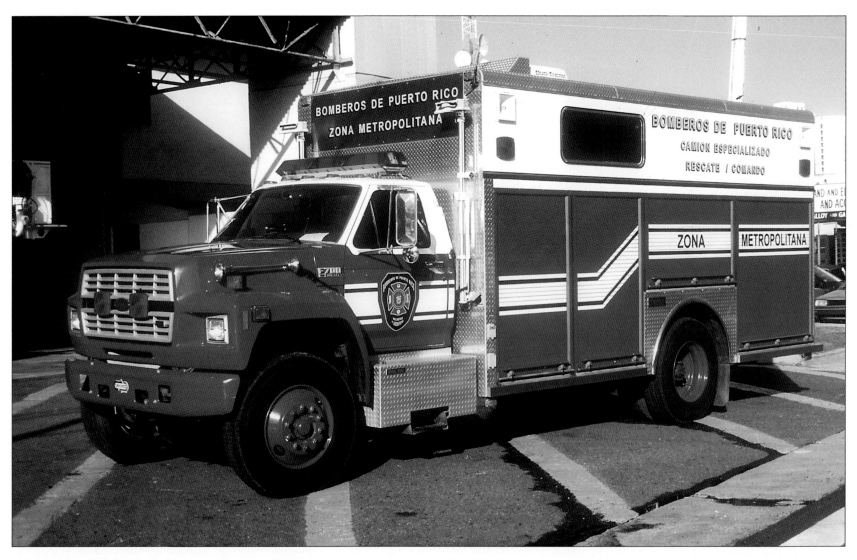

San Juan, Puerto Rico — From an Arctic delivery to a tropical one. The Bomberos de Puerto Rico purchased four identical rescue, command, and hazardous materials units built on 1992 Ford F-700 conventional chassis for the Caribbean island fire department's four protection zones. This truck is assigned to the "Zona Metropolitana" or the "Metropolitan Zone," which is responsible for the protection of the commonwealth's capital city of San Juan. All four units were equipped with 20-kilowatt generators, air cascade systems, and decontamination systems, which included electric water pumps, onboard 150-gallon water tanks, and reeled hose. Note the large air conditioning unit on the body's roof. *Photo by Joel L. Gebet*

Telford, Pennsylvania — Another Saulsbury first in 1992 was the delivery of the first Stealth engine to this small community located in the southeastern portion of the state just north of Philadelphia. The Stealth model was known for having the motor mounted behind the cab (which allowed for a more spacious and quieter cab), hydraulically actuated valves, and a color-coded "Diagrammatic" pump panel. Engine 75-1 was equipped with a 1,500-gpm pump, a 750-gallon water tank, four crosslays, and rescue-style compartmentation. *Photo by Joel L. Gebet*

Miami, Florida — The nation's largest southernmost city received its first Saulsbury unit, a walk-around haz-ardous materials unit, in 1992. Haz Mat 3 was built on a Simon-Duplex D-500 chassis. The rear section of the crew cab had a command center equipped with library, computer, cellular phone and radio bank. *Photo courtesy Saulsbury Fire Rescue*

Miami, Florida — Another view of Haz Mat 3 showing the Saulsbury custom-built compartments and the amount of equipment that could be organized, stored, and quickly accessed. Note the large and small compartments at the rear of the truck, and the roll-down awning on the side of the truck for shielding weary firefighters from the hot southern Florida sun. *Photo courtesy Saulsbury Fire Rescue*

Philadelphia, Pennsylvania — When the Philadelphia Fire Department reactivated their heavy rescue company in 1991, they turned to Saulsbury to design and build them a new vehicle capable of carrying the unit's specialized equipment. The result was this large tandem axle Spartan chassis with custom walk-in rescue body delivered in 1992. Rescue One was equipped with a 20-kilowatt generator, Will-Burt light tower, and two 12,000-pound electric winches mounted at the front and rear of the truck. Note the twin siren speakers on the front bumper. *Photo courtesy Saulsbury Fire Rescue*

Hecktown, Pennsylvania — The Hecktown Volunteer Fire Company chose Saulsbury to build their new rescue pumper in 1993. Built on a Spartan chassis, Engine 5312 was equipped with a "Diagrammatic" pump panel located inside of the crew cab area that controlled the electric over hydraulically activated valves of the engine's 1,500-gpm pump. It also carried 900 gallons of water, 100 gallons of foam, a 12-kilowatt generator, and was painted in a striking red over white over dark red paint scheme. *Photo by Joel L. Gebet*

Aberdeen, Maryland — The last of the five Saulsbury heavy rescue trucks equipped with cranes was delivered to this department located northeast of Baltimore in 1993. One of the most technically advanced rescue trucks at the time, Heavy Rescue 251 was built on a Spartan Gladiator tandem axle chassis. Its most impressive feature was its 57-foot JLG crane with a lift capacity of 14 tons. Other equipment stored in the truck's 17-compartment body included a 25-kilowatt generator, a four bottle, 6,000-psi air cascade system, a unique lift-out trench rescue pod, as well as a 20,000-pound front-mounted winch. *Photo by Joel L. Gebet*

Middletown, Pennsylvania — The Rescue Hose Company's new Engine Three was built in 1993 on a Simon-Duplex four-door chassis with raised roof. Designed with an interesting New York City-style hose bed cover, the unit was equipped with a 1,500-gpm pump and carried 720 gallons of water, 30 gallons of foam, a 10-kilowatt generator, and was painted white with a red stripe. *Photo by Joel L. Gebet*

Nanuet, New York — A Saulsbury custom-designed rescue pumper on a Simon-Duplex chassis was delivered in 1993 to the Nanuet Fire Engine Company. The unusual fully-enclosed engine was decked out with the latest features including a 1,000-gpm pump with electric over hydraulic valves that were controlled from the pump panel located in the body's first compartment, a 750-gallon water tank, a 20-kilowatt generator, and a 25-foot Will-Burt telescoping light tower. Note the engine's pre-connected lines located behind the cab and in the front bumper. *Photo by Joel L. Gebet*

New York City, New York — Saulsbury built all of the latest generation of the FDNY's six Satellite Units on 1993 Mack MR chassis. Each had storage capacity for 36 five-gallon foam pails and a spacious hose bed for carrying large diameter hose. The units' massive 4,000-gpm Stang Intelligent deluge guns, equipped with two, two-and-a-half, three, three-and-a-half, and four-inch strait bore tips, were removed from the department's older Satellite units and transferred to the new chassis. Two Akron 1,200-gpm fixed monitors were also mounted on each side of the deluge gun. *Photo by Joel L. Gebet*

New York City, New York — The first foam unit purchased new by the FDNY was this Mack MR with Saulsbury bodywork that was delivered in 1993. The Foam Tender Unit, operated by the firefighters of Engine 238 in the Greenpoint section of Brooklyn, was equipped with three separate 1,000-gallon foam tanks that allowed the unit to carry up to three different types of firefighting foam and a 200-gpm foam transfer pump. *Photo by Joel L. Gebet*

Harmony Fire Company, Mullica Hill, New Jersey — This massive rescue pumper was designed to handle almost any type of incident that a small town fire department might face. Saulsbury built the unit on a 1993 Simon-Duplex D9400 tandem axle chassis. Engine 2318's list of features included a 2,000-gpm pump, 1,000-gallon water tank, 50-gallon foam tank, Compressed Air Foam System, a 20-kilowatt generator, and a 12,000-pound electric winch. Painted white over red with a black stripe, the engine also featured an interesting mural of the fire company's older equipment and station directly above the pump panel. *Photo by Joel L. Gebet*

New York City, New York — The NYPD Emergency Services Bureau took delivery of this unique combination generator and light truck from Saulsbury in 1994 for major incidents that might take place at night or during a power outage. Built on a Freightliner FL70 chassis with a two-door cab, the unit's walk-around body carried enough equipment to make an electric company jealous. The unit's direct drive generator was rated at an amazing 100 kilowatts and inside the compartments were five electrical cable reels, 27 portable electric cable reels, 23 electrical junction boxes, 80 portable floodlights, and 40 portable floodlight tripods. Stationed with Emergency Services Squad 7 in Brooklyn, this truck was also equipped with two Will-Burt 28-foot light towers that could pan and tilt and that were rated at 9,000 watts each. *Photo by Joel L. Gebet*

Miami, Florida — Miami Fire Rescue received Foam 3, a Simon-Duplex Stealth Series engine from Saulsbury in 1994. Operating along with the department's 1992 Saulsbury Haz Mat unit, the engine had a 1,250-gpm pump with a "Diagrammatic" pump panel and carried 40 gallons of Class A foam and 60 gallons of Class B foam. Note the unit's unusual bus-style doors for firefighters riding in the crew cab area. *Photo courtesy Saulsbury Fire Rescue*

Rodney-Aldborough, Ontario, Canada — Several Saulsbury vehicles made their way "north of the border" to Canada throughout the 1990s. One of the largest vehicles delivered was this "Mohawk" series tanker built on a 1994 Freightliner FL80 chassis. Tanker One has a non-painted stainless steel body equipped with a 1,000-gpm pump, a 2,500-gallon water tank, and two crosslays. *Photo courtesy Saulsbury Fire Rescue*

A rear view of Tanker One shows the unit's 10-inch quick dump valve and the hose bed designed to accommodate a folding water tank, a 35-foot extension ladder, two lengths of hard suction hose, and 500 feet of 2 1/2-inch hose. *Photo courtesy Saulsbury Fire Rescue*

Elmont, New York — This nifty little special services unit was the only vehicle Saulsbury ever built using the rear-engine Spartan GT-1 chassis. Unit 709 was delivered to the Elmont Fire Department in 1994 and was equipped with a 6,000-watt light tower, 20-kilowatt generator, and a seven bottle air cascade system. Note the mural of the octopus on the crew cab door holding the different types of firefighting equipment carried on the truck. *Photo by Joel L. Gebet*

New Egypt Fire Company, Plumsted Township, New Jersey — This small fire company protecting a town located in the Pine Barrens of southern New Jersey purchased this impressive pumper-tanker from Saulsbury in 1994. Built on a Peterbuilt 357 Conventional chassis, the large tanker has a 1,500-gpm pump, 3,500-gallon water tank, a 12-inch rear quick dump and two roll-up doors on each side of the body. Note the large mural of a camel pulling a hand-pumper in an oasis in the Egyptian desert that pokes fun at the fire company's name. *Photo by Dermot Scales*

Londonderry, Pennsylvania — First due at the infamous Three Mile Island nuclear power plant located just south of the state capital of Harrisburg is the Londonderry Fire Company, which received this large Saulsbury tanker in 1994. Built on a Spartan Gladiator chassis, Tanker 54 had a 1,750-gpm pump and carried 3,000 gallons of water. Note the large roll-up door behind the pump panel and the small mural of Three Mile Island on the crew cab door. *Photo by Joel L. Gebet*

Salem, New Jersey—While high-pressure pumpers were common during the 1950s and 1960s, they were very rare when Saulsbury delivered three of these type of engines in 1994 and 1995. The first was delivered to the Liberty Fire Company in 1994. Engine 6-2 was built on a Simon-Duplex D9400 short-wheelbase chassis and was equipped with a high-pressure pump rated at 1,000-psi that carried 1,000 gallons of water. The unit was painted black over red with a black stripe. Note the "John Bean" high pressure "gun-style" nozzle mounted on the body just above the pump panel. *Photo by Joel L. Gebet*

Ronkonkoma, New York — The Ronkonkoma Fire Department placed two of these unique high pressure "attack" engines in service in 1995. Built on short wheelbase Freightliner FL80 chassis, the engines were equipped with high pressure pumps that were rated at approximately 70-gpm and 750-gallon water tanks. Again, note the high pressure "gun style" nozzle mounted on the body just behind the pump panel. *Photo by Joel L. Gebet*

West Tuckerton Fire Company, Little Egg Harbor Township, New Jersey — This interesting short-wheelbase engine was delivered to this coastal New Jersey town located just north of Atlantic City in 1995. Equipped with a pump panel located inside of the raised-roof crew cab area, Engine 7101 had a 1,500-gpm pump, carried 1,000 gallons of water, and was painted in an unusual white over silver over white paint scheme with red and blue stripes. Note the mural on the middle compartment door that depicts *Casper the Friendly Ghost* using a hose to battle both the infamous Jersey Devil and a fully involved house fire. *Photo by Joel L. Gebet*

ALCAN Corporation, Oswego, New York — Another rare Saulsbury delivery to an industrial fire department was made in 1995 to ALCAN's Oswego Aluminum Rolling Plant Complex. Built on a short-wheelbase HME chassis for operations inside some of the plant's buildings, the engine had a 1,250-gpm pump and carried 300 gallons of water and 100 gallons of foam. An Ansul 150-pound dry chemical system was mounted in the rear compartment below the engine's hose bed. *Photo courtesy Saulsbury Fire Rescue*

West Chester, Pennsylvania — The Good Will Fire Company received this Saulsbury pumper with rescue-style compartments in 1995. Built on a Spartan Gladiator chassis, the most unique features of Engine 52-2 were its two pre-piped deck guns visible just behind the cab. The engine was equipped with a 2,000-gpm pump, 750-gallon water tank, 40-gallon Class A foam tank, 40-gallon Class B foam tank, and a 12-kilowatt generator. Engine 52-2 was painted white with green stripes. *Photo by Joel L. Gebet*

Applegarth Fire Company, Monroe Township, New Jersey — Possibly one of the smallest Class A engines that Saulsbury ever built was also one of the first of its "Scorpion" series of engines. Delivered in 1995, the engine was specially designed by the fire company to be able to access small roadways in the townships' numerous industrial parks as well as to fit inside its extremely cramped fire station. The result was this very well-equipped Spartan chassis with a rear-mounted 1,250-gpm pump, 500-gallon water tank, 15-kilowatt generator, 6,000-watt Will-Burt light tower, and a remote control deck gun mounted directly above the left rear compartment; the same compartment where Engine 57-1's pump panel was located. At 24 feet, 8 inches, the engine was shorter than many of the rescue bodies Saulsbury built. *Photo by Joel L. Gebet*

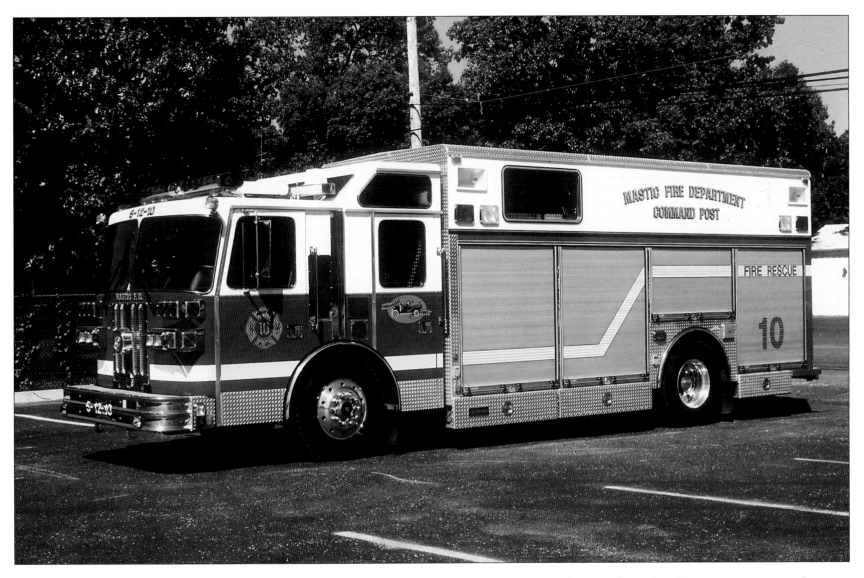

Mastic, New York — While Saulsbury is known for building the lion's share of its bodies on custom chassis produced by such manufacturers as American LaFrance, Hahn, HME, Mack, Simon-Duplex, and Spartan, the company would, from time to time, build a unit on a chassis they had rarely, if ever, used. Such was the case with this combination rescue truck and command post built on a Sutphen chassis in 1995. Saulsbury used only one other Sutphen chassis, and that was also for a heavy rescue truck delivered to Bethesda, North Carolina in 1991. *Photo by Joel L. Gebet*

Port Penn, Delaware — This small, historic Delaware town's fire department has been a very loyal Saulsbury customer over the past 30 years, ordering no less than four different vehicles. The biggest of them all was this Simon-Duplex tandem axle tanker that was delivered in 1996. Tanker 29 had a 2,000-gpm pump with three crosslays and carried 2,500 gallons of water. *Photo by Joel L. Gebet*

East Orange, New Jersey — Saulsbury delivered an interesting combination of an HME tandem axle chassis with a 50-foot Tele-Squirt to this northern New Jersey city in 1996. Equipped with a 1,750-gpm pump with two crosslays, and a 750-gallon water tank, it was assigned to Engine 2, which (as noted on the cab above the windshield) was originally known as "Eastern Hose" when the department was first formed in the 19th Century. *Photo by Joel L. Gebet*

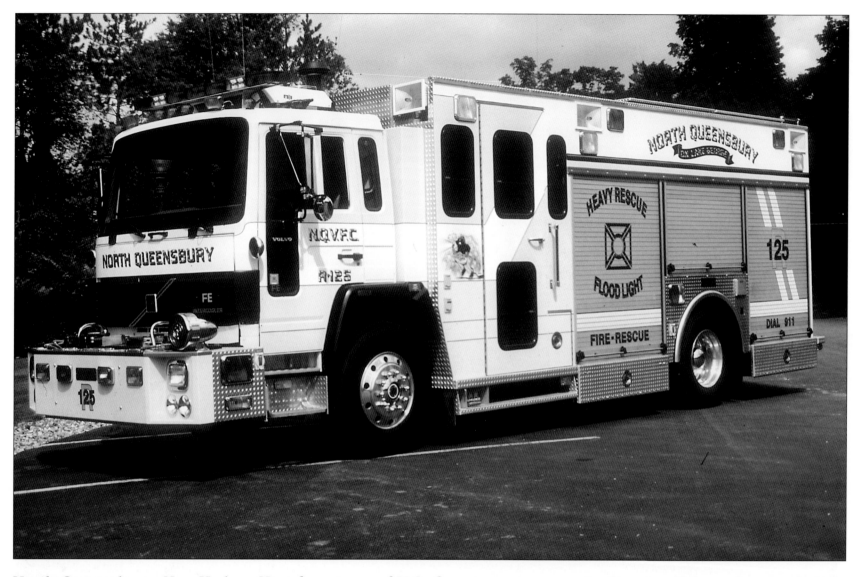

North Queensbury, New York — Very few pieces of U.S. fire apparatus were built using Volvo cab-over chassis like the one this fire department (located on the banks of the famous Lake George in northern New York State) chose for their Heavy Rescue 125. Saulsbury built this unusual heavy rescue and floodlight unit in 1996 and equipped it with a 48-kilowatt generator, two 6,000-watt Will-Burt light towers, and an extended front bumper with hydraulic extrication tools and a 5,000-pound winch. Note the unusual crew cab area built into the body, which was capable of carrying 10 firefighters. *Photo by Joel L. Gebet*

Star Petroleum Refining Company LTD., Thailand — Rare times three is this nifty little mobile command vehicle, one of the very few foreign industrial fire department deliveries in Saulsbury history. It was made even more rare by the customer's choice of chassis, the Volvo FL7 with right hand side drive! Delivered during 1996, the unit was equipped with roll-up doors, an air-conditioned body, and a rear-mounted mast for a video camera to record incidents. Note the unit's Thai lettering. *Photo by John Greible*

A view of the left side of the command unit showing its interesting cab and the entrance to the vehicle's body. Note the lettering on this side of the truck is in English. *Photo by John Greible*

Lancaster County, Pennsylvania — This massive hazardous materials unit was delivered to this all-volunteer team that protects this county that is famous for its large Amish population and its farms. Built on a 1996 Simon-Duplex 9200 chassis, Haz Mat 2-9-1's 26-foot walk-in body was equipped with a command post area accessible from a door with a fold-down diamond plate staircase (visible just behind the body's first window), a 24-kilowatt PTO generator, and a roll-down awning. The unit was painted in an interesting color scheme of all white with orange and blue stripes. *Photo by Joel L. Gebet*

Clinton, New Jersey — When the Hummer (the civilian version of the U.S. military's Humvee) debuted in the mid-1990s, numerous fire apparatus manufacturers saw it as the perfect base to build brush and small rescue trucks on. Soon after they were released, several fire departments jumped at the opportunity to add these rugged, go-anywhere vehicles to their rosters but due to their expense, not very many have been built. The Clinton Fire Department ordered one of the only two Hummers with Saulsbury bodywork in 1997. Equipped

with a rear-mounted 350-gpm PTO pump and a 200-gallon water tank, Unit 45-81 had a 200-foot booster reel and a 150-foot, 1 1/2-inch attack line. *Photo by Joel L. Gebet*

This rear view of the Clinton Hummer shows the rear mount pump and the separate diesel engine that powers it as well as its booster line. The 1 1/2-inch attack line was stored in one of the transverse compartments on top of the body. The department affectionately nicknamed the brush unit "We Fear No Deer." *Photo by Joel L. Gebet*

Basalt and Rural Fire District, El Jebel, Colorado — This massive pumper-tanker was delivered to this fire department located northwest of Aspen in 1997. Built on a Spartan Gladiator chassis, Tender 42 had an unusual 1,500-gpm rear-mount pump with the pump panel located in a compartment below the hose bed. It was also equipped with a Compressed Air Foam System and carried 2,200 gallons of water. Note the three pre-connected hose lines directly behind the cab. *Photo by Dennis J. Maag*

A view of the rear of Tender 42 showing its unique pump panel and intake and discharge arrangement. *Photo by Dennis J. Maag*

Fair Lawn, New Jersey — The first Stealth pumper to see service in New Jersey was built on a Simon-Duplex D8400 chassis and delivered to the Fair Lawn Fire Department's Company 1 in 1997. Engine 971 was equipped with a 1,250-gpm pump with a "Diagrammatic" pump panel and carried 750 gallons of water, 40 gallons of foam, and a telescoping light tower. *Photo by Joel L. Gebet*

A view of the rear of Engine 971 showing the unit's unique intake and discharge configuration while operating at a multiple alarm structure fire in October 2002. *Photo by Joel L. Gebet*

New York City, New York — The largest heavy rescue units operated to date by the FDNY were placed in service in 1997. Measuring in at just over 37-feet long, the five rescues were built on HME Stubby cabs and chassis. Each was equipped with a 25-kilowatt generator, a cab-roof-mounted Will-Burt light tower, and pike poles mounted outside the unit just behind the crew cab for quick access. *Photo by John A. Calderone*

New York City, New York — While most people would probably not think of New York City as having large areas of undeveloped land, several areas within the city's outlying boroughs actually fit this description. With that comes the possibility of serious brush fires and to help prevent them the FDNY ordered five of these heavy-duty brush trucks from Saulsbury in 1997. Built on International 4800 four-wheel drive chassis, the units, known locally as BFUs (brush fire units) were equipped with 500-gpm rear-mounted pumps capable of pump-and-roll operations and carrying 500 gallons of water. Note the black steel roll bars surrounding the cab of BFU-2, quartered with Engine 166 in Staten Island. *Photo by Joel L. Gebet*

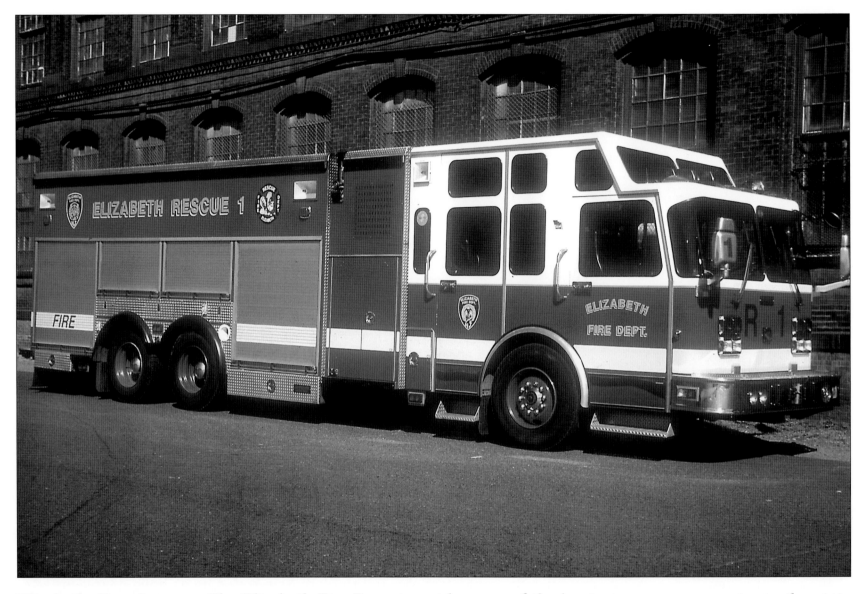

Elizabeth, New Jersey — The Elizabeth Fire Department has one of the busiest rescue companies in the state and operated one of the largest rescue vehicles in the New York City Metropolitan area. Measuring in at just over 38 feet long, Rescue One was built by Saulsbury on a 1998 Spartan Baron mid-engine chassis with a 3-door cab. The 24-foot walk-in body was equipped with a 25-kilowatt generator and had front- and rear-mounted 12,000–pound winches. *Photo by Joel L. Gebet*

Weldon Fire Company, Glenside, Pennsylvania — Engine 300 is one of a pair of identical engines operated by this fire company located in the suburbs just north of Philadelphia. Built on 1998 Spartan Gladiator chassis, the engines had a very unique fully electronic pump panel area with three crosslays arranged vertically to the left of the panel. The engines were each equipped with 2,000-gpm pumps, 500-gallon water tanks, and 50-gallon foam tanks. *Photo by Joel L. Gebet*

New York City, New York — Once again following the FDNY's lead with Saulsbury-built vehicles, the NYPD received three of these Emergency Support Vehicles (known locally as ESVs) in 1998, units that are very similar to the two Tactical Support Vehicles Saulsbury delivered to the FDNY that same year. Built on International 4700 "Lo-Profile" chassis, they were equipped with Zodiac boats, small 6,000-pound Auto Cranes for removing the boat from the truck, 15-kilowatt generators, and a roof-mounted 1,500-watt Will-Burt light tower. The vehicles also carried extra SCUBA equipment, an electric Hurst Tool, and special air bags capable of saving the life of a person threatening to jump off of a building or other tall structure. Note the outriggers just behind the cab door used for stabilizing the unit when operating the crane. *Photo by Joel L. Gebet*

Metro West Fire District, Ballwin, Missouri — To say that this department spared no expense when ordering this massive heavy rescue truck would be an understatement! Built on a 1998 Spartan Gladiator chassis, Rescue 3316's list of impressive features included a rear-steering tag axle, a 90-watt PTO generator, two Will-Burt 9,000-kilowatt light towers, an air compressor, a four-bottle 6,000-psi air cascade system, and an IFEX high-pressure water fire extinguishing system. The unit was painted bright yellow with a white stripe. *Photo by Dennis J. Maag*

Aberdeen Township, New Jersey — Aberdeen Fire District One received this very uniquely designed Saulsbury aerial apparatus in 1998. Built on a Simon-Duplex cab and chassis, the unit featured a 2,000-gpm pump, a 500-gallon water tank, and a 50-foot Tele-Squirt. What made this engine so unique was that the pump panel was located at the rear of the unit next to the control panel for the Tele-Squirt. It was the first such unit built by Saulsbury and, quite possibly, the first such unit in the entire fire apparatus industry. *Photo by Joel L. Gebet*

A view of the rear of the unit shows the very interesting layout for the unit's operator with the pump panel at the left and the Tele-Squirt controls at the right. *Photo by Joel L. Gebet*

108

Nanuet, New York — Saulsbury and its dealers also sold Ladder Towers Incorporated aerial products from 1994 through 1998 in a relationship similar to the one Saulsbury had with American LaFrance from 1978 to 1984. The result was several interesting pieces of fire apparatus with Saulsbury bodies and LTI aerials, such as this 75-foot ladder tower delivered to this town located northwest of New York City in 1998. Built on a Simon-Duplex chassis, Tower 8, the only Saulsbury/LTI combination built with an LTI ladder tower was also equipped with a 1,500-gpm pump, 300-gallon water tank, and 20-kilowatt generator. Note the single rear tire, which is for the unit's steering tag axle. *Photo by Joel L. Gebet*

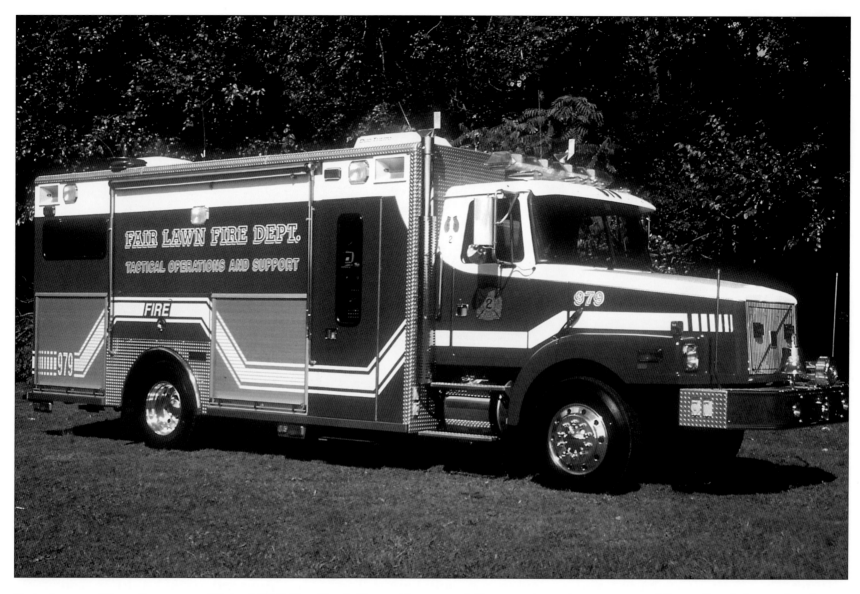

Fair Lawn, New Jersey — This 1998 Tactical Operations and Support unit was one of four Saulsbury-built vehicles operated by this northern New Jersey fire department. Unit 979, built on a unique Volvo WG42 conventional chassis, was operated as a communications and air cascade unit. The six-bottle air cascade system was mounted in the rear of the vehicle, while the communications portion was accessed through the truck's side door. Equipped with a computer, fax machine, five cellular phones and a 12-radio console, the unit also featured an extendible radio antenna and a roll-down awning. *Photo by Joel L. Gebet*

New York City, New York — The newest version of trucks designed to carry the NYPD Emergency Services Unit's arsenal of SWAT and other specialized equipment were a fleet of 11 of these Mack MR heavy rescue style vehicles delivered between 1998 and 2003 that were painted all white with blue stripes. Shown above is Truck 6, a 1999 model stationed in the Bay Ridge section of Brooklyn. All were equipped with 24-kilowatt generators, 20-foot, 6,000-watt Will-Burt light towers, and electric and hydraulic Hurst Tools. Note the compartment built near the roof in the middle of the rescue body under the "Emergency" lettering. *Photo by Joel L. Gebet*

East Hanover, New Jersey — The only Saulsbury apparatus built with a Snozzle articulating boom was delivered to this northern New Jersey town in 1999. The 50-foot articulating Snozzle boom, equipped with an additional piercing nozzle, was manufactured by Crash Rescue Equipment Services in Dallas, Texas. These booms are rarely utilized on municipal fire apparatus and are mostly mounted on airport crash fire rescue vehicles. Engine 863 was also equipped with a 1,500-gpm pump and a 750-gallon water tank. Note the lack of intakes and discharges on the pump panel, which were all located on the officer's side of the truck for the safety of the pump operator. *Photo by Joel L. Gebet*

Westbury, New York — This Long Island fire department operated the only Saulsbury-built unit with an Aerial Innovations product. Ladder 963's 105-foot aerial ladder was mated to a large 2000 Spartan Gladiator tandem rear axle chassis whose Saulsbury body was also equipped with a 10-kilowatt generator. Note the two diamond plate boxes on the truck's bumper designed to house twin electrical cord reels. *Photo by Joel L. Gebet*

Fort Lee, New Jersey — Saulsbury delivered this interesting top-mount engine to this city, located at the foot of the George Washington Bridge directly across from New York City, in 2000. Built on a Spartan Gladiator chassis, Engine Two (painted in an interesting color scheme of white over red with white and black stripes) was equipped with a 1,750-gpm pump and carried 750 gallons of water and 50 gallons of foam. Note the four lights at the top right corner of the cab that alerted firefighters to the level of the engine's water tank. *Photo by Joel L. Gebet*

Fair Harbor, New York — Protecting this tiny resort community located on New York's Fire Island was this very unusual short-wheelbase engine delivered by Saulsbury in 2001. Built on an International 4900 four-wheel-drive chassis, Engine 3-16-7 is equipped with a 1,250-gpm pump and a large rear-mounted hose reel capable of holding 2,500 feet of five-inch hose. The engine, patterned after a similar Saulsbury unit delivered to Sister Bay, Wisconsin, was designed as a water supply truck capable of drafting directly from the Atlantic Ocean. Note the large mural on the body of the engine of Neptune holding a hose. *Photo by Joel L. Gebet*

New York City, New York — The third generation of Saulsbury-built FDNY hazardous materials units was this huge tandem axle unit delivered during 2001, the largest hazmat vehicle ever operated by the FDNY. Built on a two-door Mack MR chassis, the 26-foot walk-in body had an air-conditioned command center in the front portion complete with a weather center, a laboratory, a 30-kilowatt generator, and every conceivable piece of equipment for handling a major hazardous materials incident. Note the diamond plate box on the cab roof that provides protection for the 15-foot, 6,000-watt Will-Burt light tower. *Photo by Joel L. Gebet.*

Coram, New York — Looking more like a fire engine found in an industrial fire department rather than a municipal one is this impressive tandem axle pumper delivered by Saulsbury in 2001. Engine 3, built on a Spartan Gladiator chassis, had a 2,000-gpm pump with top-mounted pump panel, 1,400-gallon water tank and two separate foam tanks carrying 200 gallons of Class A foam and 500 gallons of Class B foam. The unit also carried 3,000 feet of five-inch hose — but its most interesting feature was its huge Williams "Hot Shot II" monitor capable of flowing an unbelievable 4,000 gallons of water and foam per minute! *Photo by Joel L. Gebet*

Centereach, New York — The Centereach Fire Department's Emergency Company recevied the last of three massive Saulsbury-built heavy rescue trucks delivered to fire departments on New York's Long Island between 1999-2001. The walk-in units were all built on tandem axle Spartan Gladiator chassis. Rescue 5-5-4's 22-foot body was equipped with a 35-kilowatt PTO generator, five bottle, 6,000-psi cascade system, 15-foot, 9,000-watt light tower, and a 15,000-pound front-mounted winch. The other two rescues were delivered to Hauppauge and Wantagh. *Photo by Joel L. Gebet*

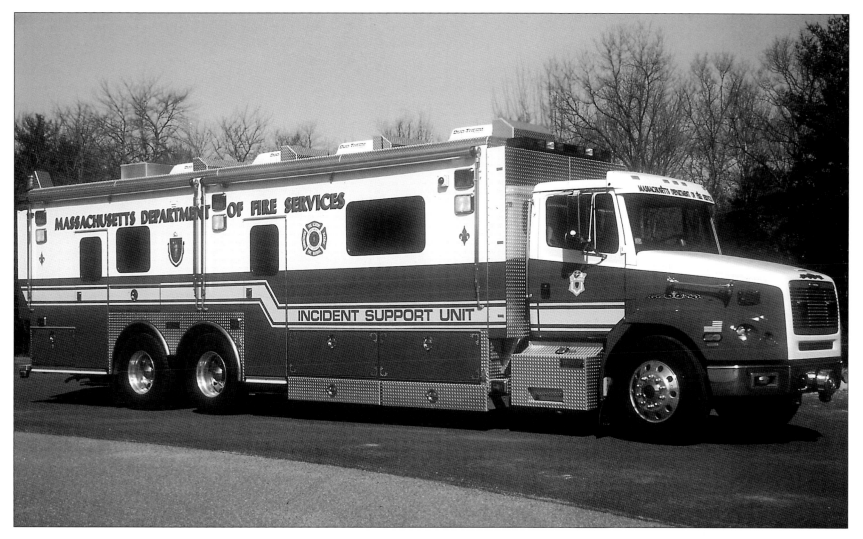

Massachusetts Department of Fire Services — While it might appear to be another Saulsbury-built heavy rescue, this gigantic truck is actually an office on wheels. Utilized as a mobile command post for major incidents across the Commonwealth of Massachusetts, the 40-foot long Incident Support Unit was built on a 2001 Freightliner FL112 chassis. The 29-foot Saulsbury body was equipped with numerous mobile and portable radios, three computer workstations, a 30-foot mast with a video camera to record incidents, a conference area in the front of the body, and two generators; a 35-kilowatt PTO and a 12.5-kilowatt unit utilized as a backup power supply for the unit's computer system. Note the four air-conditioning units mounted on the top of the body. *Photo by Joel L. Gebet*

Whiting, New Jersey — One of the more unique deliveries Saulsbury produced during 2002 was this four-wheel-drive rescue pumper built on a Peterbilt PB330 chassis. Engine 3303's list of features included a 750-gpm pump with a foam system, 450 gallons of water, 50 gallons of Class A foam, and a 10-kilowatt generator. Note the Will-Burt light tower mounted directly above the pump panel and the winch mounted in the front bumper. *Photo by Joel L. Gebet*

Tallahassee, Florida — As part of its purchase by Federal Signal, Saulsbury would become responsible for building the bodywork for all new orders of the company's 100-foot Bronto Skylifts in 2002. One of the first to be delivered was this interesting white over red truck, the first Bronto Skylift with a boom painted all red. Built on an E-One Cyclone II chassis, the truck was equipped with a 2,000-gpm pump, a 300-gallon water tank, a 20-gallon foam tank, a nine-kilowatt generator, and two crosslays. Note the compartment built into the cab of the unit behind the driver's door designed for easy access to the medical equipment carried on the truck. *Photo by Joel L. Gebet*

New York City, New York — These are the newest generation of the two Tactical Support Units (known locally as TSUs) operated by the FDNY for responses to multiple alarm fires, SCUBA rescues, building collapses, and other major incidents. Built by Saulsbury on 2002 International 4800 4x4 chassis, both were equipped with 28-kilowatt generators, 9,000-watt light towers, Zumro rescue boats, and small cranes for removing and placing the boats into the water. These trucks recently replaced two identical units that were built in 1998, one of which was destroyed in the attack on the World Trade Center on September 11, 2001, while the other is held in reserve. *Photo by Joel L. Gebet*

A view of the officer's side showing the unit's crane, rated at 6,000 pounds, and the light tower, which is recessed inside of the diamond plate box behind the cab. Note the small outrigger at the rear of the vehicle used for stability when the crane is operated. *Photo by Joel L. Gebet*

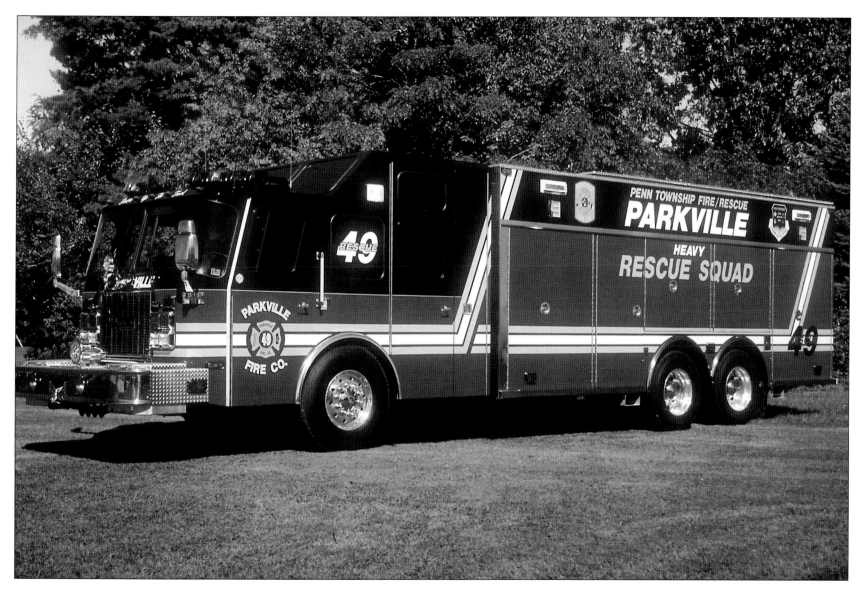

Penn Township, Pennsylvania — This impressive 24-foot walk-around heavy rescue squad was placed in service by the Parkville Fire Company in 2002. Built on an E-One Cyclone II tandem axle chassis, Rescue 49 featured a 48-kilowatt generator, a 12,000-watt Will-Burt light tower, and a four-cylinder 6,000-psi air cascade system. The rescue was painted black over red with white and yellow stripes. Note the "Roto-Ray" warning light mounted below the front windshield. *Photo by Joel L. Gebet*

Hillsborough County, Florida — The largest vehicle ever built by Saulsbury and one of the largest heavy rescue trucks to see service in the United States was the Hillsborough County Fire Department's Heavy Rescue 11. At over 43 feet long, this enormous rescue was built on a 2002 E-One Cyclone II tandem axle chassis. Along with every conceivable type of rescue tool, its 30-foot walk-around body was equipped with 40-kilowatt generator, a 15-foot, 6,000-watt Will-Burt light tower, and a 10-foot Avon inflatable rescue boat. Painted in a unique white and lime green color scheme, the rescue was stationed in the community of Brandon located just east of Tampa. Note the bars that protected the windows on the top of the cab. *Photo by Joel L. Gebet*

New York City, New York — It is appropriate that two of the last "true" Saulsbury deliveries were to the city that helped make the company the success it was to become. Both of the trucks were assigned to the NYPD's Emergency Services Unit 4 in the Bronx and included Truck 4, a 2002 Mack MR heavy rescue-type vehicle and MALT-4 (short for "Multi-Area-Lighting-Truck"), a light and generator truck built on a 2002 International 7600 chassis. MALT-4, whose 18-foot body was equipped with a massive 108-kilowatt generator and twin 9,000-watt Will-Burt light towers, was donated to New York City by the French aircraft manufacturer Airbus to assist in the city's recovery efforts after the attack on the World Trade Center complex on September 11, 2001. *Photo by Joel L. Gebet*

Over its 47 years in business, Saulsbury used several different versions of name plates to identify the vehicles it built, including these four types used during the 1970s to 2003. Clockwise from top left photo: early-1970s until early-1980s; early-1980s until early-1990s; mid-1990s until 2001; early-1990s until 2003. *Photos by Joel L. Gebet*

AMERICAN CULTURE

- *Coca-Cola: A History in Photographs 1930-1969* ISBN 1-882256-46-8
- *Coca-Cola: Its Vehicles in Photographs 1930-1969* ISBN 1-882256-47-6
- *Phillips 66 1945-1954 Photo Archive* ISBN 1-882256-42-5

AUTOMOTIVE

- *AMX Photo Archive: From Concept to Reality* ISBN 1-58388-062-3
- *Auburn Automobiles 1900-1936 Photo Archive* ISBN 1-58388-093-3
- *Camaro 1967-2000 Photo Archive* ISBN 1-58388-032-1
- *Checker Cab Co. Photo History* ISBN 1-58388-100-X
- *Chevrolet Station Wagons 1946-1966 Photo Archive* ISBN 1-58388-069-0
- *Classic American Limousines 1955-2000 Photo Archive* ISBN 1-58388-041-0
- *Corvair by Chevrolet Experimental & Production Cars 1957-1969, Ludvigsen Library Series* ISBN 1-58388-058-5
- *Corvette The Exotic Experimental Cars, Ludvigsen Library Series* ISBN 1-58388-017-8
- *Corvette Prototypes & Show Cars Photo Album* ISBN 1-882256-77-8
- *Early Ford V-8s 1932-1942 Photo Album* ISBN 1-882256-97-2
- *Ferrari- The Factory Maranello's Secrets 1950-1975, Ludvigsen Library Series* ISBN 1-58388-085-2
- *Ford Postwar Flatheads 1946-1953 Photo Archive* ISBN 1-58388-080-1
- *Ford Station Wagons 1929-1991 Photo History* ISBN 1-58388-103-4
- *Imperial 1955-1963 Photo Archive* ISBN 1-882256-22-0
- *Imperial 1964-1968 Photo Archive* ISBN 1-882256-23-9
- *Javelin Photo Archive: From Concept to Reality* ISBN 1-58388-071-2
- *Lincoln Motor Cars 1920-1942 Photo Archive* ISBN 1-882256-57-3
- *Lincoln Motor Cars 1946-1960 Photo Archive* ISBN 1-882256-58-1
- *Nash 1936-1957 Photo Archive* ISBN 1-58388-086-0
- *Packard Motor Cars 1935-1942 Photo Archive* ISBN 1-882256-44-1
- *Packard Motor Cars 1946-1958 Photo Archive* ISBN 1-882256-45-X
- *Pontiac Dream Cars, Show Cars & Prototypes 1928-1998 Photo Album* ISBN 1-882256-93-X
- *Pontiac Firebird Trans-Am 1969-1999 Photo Album* ISBN 1-882256-95-6
- *Pontiac Firebird 1967-2000 Photo History* ISBN 1-58388-028-3
- *Rambler 1950-1969 Photo Archive* ISBN 1-58388-078-X
- *Stretch Limousines 1928-2001 Photo Archive* ISBN 1-58388-070-4
- *Studebaker 1933-1942 Photo Archive* ISBN 1-882256-24-7
- *Studebaker Hawk 1956-1964 Photo Archive* ISBN 1-58388-094-1
- *Studebaker Lark 1959-1966 Photo Archive* ISBN 1-58388-107-7
- *Ultimate Corvette Trivia Challenge* ISBN 1-58388-035-6

BUSES

- *Buses of ACF Photo Archive* ISBN 1-58388-101-8
- *Buses of Motor Coach Industries 1932-2000 Photo Archive* ISBN 1-58388-039-9
- *Fageol & Twin Coach Buses 1922-1956 Photo Archive* ISBN 1-58388-075-5
- *Flxible Intercity Buses 1924-1970 Photo Archive* ISBN 1-58388-108-5
- *Flxible Transit Buses 1953-1995 Photo Archive* ISBN 1-58388-053-4
- *GM Intercity Coaches 1944-1980 Photo Archive* ISBN 1-58388-099-2
- *Greyhound Buses 1914-2000 Photo Archive* ISBN 1-58388-027-5
- *Mack® Buses 1900-1960 Photo Archive** ISBN 1-58388-020-8
- *Prevost Buses 1924-2002 Photo Archive* ISBN 1-58388-083-6
- *Trailways Buses 1936-2001 Photo Archive* ISBN 1-58388-029-1
- *Trolley Buses 1913-2001 Photo Archive* ISBN 1-58388-057-7
- *Yellow Coach Buses 1923-1943 Photo Archive* ISBN 1-58388-054-2

EMERGENCY VEHICLES

- *The American Ambulance 1900-2002: An Illustrated History* ISBN 1-58388-081-X
- *American Funeral Vehicles 1883-2003 Illustrated History* ISBN 1-58388-104-2
- *American LaFrance 700 Series 1945-1952 Photo Archive* ISBN 1-882256-90-5
- *American LaFrance 700 Series 1945-1952 Photo Archive Volume 2* ISBN 1-58388-025-9
- *American LaFrance 700 & 800 Series 1953-1958 Photo Archive* ISBN 1-882256-91-3
- *American LaFrance 900 Series 1958-1964 Photo Archive* ISBN 1-58388-002-X
- *Classic Seagrave 1935-1951 Photo Archive* ISBN 1-58388-034-8
- *Crown Firecoach 1951-1985 Photo Archive* ISBN 1-58388-047-X
- *Fire Chief Cars 1900-1997 Photo Album* ISBN 1-882256-87-5
- *Hahn Fire Apparatus 1923-1990 Photo Archive* ISBN 1-58388-077-1
- *Heavy Rescue Trucks 1931-2000 Photo Gallery* ISBN 1-58388-045-3
- *Imperial Fire Apparatus 1969-1976 Photo Archive* ISBN 1-58388-091-7
- *Industrial and Private Fire Apparatus 1925-2001 Photo Archive* ISBN 1-58388-049-6
- *Los Angeles City Fire Apparatus 1953-1999 Photo Archive* ISBN 1-58388-012-7
- *Mack Model C Fire Trucks 1957-1967 Photo Archive** ISBN 1-58388-014-3
- *Mack Model L Fire Trucks 1940-1954 Photo Archive** ISBN 1-882256-86-7
- *Maxim Fire Apparatus 1914-1989 Photo Archive* ISBN 1-58388-050-X
- *Navy & Marine Corps Fire Apparatus 1836 -2000 Photo Gallery* ISBN 1-58388-031-3
- *Pierre Thibault Ltd. Fire Apparatus 1918-1990 Photo Archive* ISBN 1-58388-074-7
- *Pirsch Fire Apparatus 1890-1991 Photo Archive* ISBN 1-58388-082-8
- *Police Cars: Restoring, Collecting & Showing America's Finest Sedans* ISBN 1-58388-046-1
- *Saulsbury Fire Rescue Apparatus 1956-2003 Photo Archive* ISBN 1-58388-106-9
- *Seagrave 70th Anniversary Series Photo Archive* ISBN 1-58388-001-1
- *TASC Fire Apparatus 1946-1985 Photo Archive* ISBN 1-58388-065-8
- *Volunteer & Rural Fire Apparatus Photo Gallery* ISBN 1-58388-005-4
- *W.S. Darley & Co. Fire Apparatus 1908-2000 Photo Archive* ISBN 1-58388-061-5
- *Ward LaFrance Fire Trucks 1918-1978 Photo Archive* ISBN 1-58388-013-5
- *Wildland Fire Apparatus 1940-2001 Photo Gallery* ISBN 1-58388-056-9
- *Young Fire Equipment 1932-1991 Photo Archive* ISBN 1-58388-015-1

RACING

- *Chaparral Can-Am Racing Cars from Texas, Ludvigsen Library Series* ISBN 1-58388-066-6
- *Cunningham Sports Cars, Ludvigsen Library Series* ISBN 1-58388-109-3
- *Drag Racing Funny Cars of the 1960s Photo Archive* ISBN 1-58388-097-6
- *Drag Racing Funny Cars of the 1970s Photo Archive* ISBN 1-58388-068-2
- *El Mirage Impressions: Dry Lakes Land Speed Racing* ISBN 1-58388-059-3
- *GT40 Photo Archive* ISBN 1-882256-64-6
- *Indy Cars of the 1950s, Ludvigsen Library Series* ISBN 1-58388-018-6
- *Indy Cars of the 1960s, Ludvigsen Library Series* ISBN 1-58388-052-6
- *Indy Cars of the 1970s, Ludvigsen Library Series* ISBN 1-58388-098-4
- *Indianapolis Racing Cars of Frank Kurtis 1941-1963 Photo Archive* ISBN 1-58388-026-7
- *Juan Manuel Fangio World Champion Driver Series Photo Album* ISBN 1-58388-008-9

More Great Titles From Iconografix

All Iconografix books are available from direct mail specialty book dealers and bookstores worldwide, or can be ordered from the publisher. For book trade and distribution information or to add your name to our mailing list and receive a **FREE CATALOG** contact:

Iconografix,
PO Box 446, Dept BK
Hudson, WI, 54016

Telephone: (715) 381-9755,
(800) 289-3504 (USA),
Fax: (715) 381-9756

*This product is sold under license from Mack Trucks, Inc. Mack is a registered Trademark of Mack Trucks, Inc. All rights reserved.

- *Lost Race Tracks Treasures of Automobile Racing* ISBN 1-58388-084-4
- *Mario Andretti World Champion Driver Series Photo Album* ISBN 1-58388-009-7
- *Mercedes-Benz 300SL Racing Cars 1952-1953, Ludvigsen Library Series* ISBN 1-58388-067-4
- *Novi V-8 Indy Cars 1941-1965, Ludvigsen Library Series* ISBN 1-58388-037-2
- *Porsche Spyders Type 550 1953-1956, Ludvigsen Library Series* ISBN 1-58388-092-5
- *Sebring 12-Hour Race 1970 Photo Archive* ISBN 1-882256-20-4
- *Vanderbilt Cup Race 1936 & 1937 Photo Archive* ISBN 1-882256-66-2

RAILWAYS

- *Chicago, St. Paul, Minneapolis & Omaha Railway 1880-1940 Photo Archive* ISBN 1-882256-67-0
- *Chicago & North Western Railway 1975-1995 Photo Archive* ISBN 1-882256-76-X
- *Great Northern Railway 1945-1970 Volume 2 Photo Archive* ISBN 1-882256-79-4
- *Great Northern Railway Ore Docks of Lake Superior Photo Archive* ISBN 1-58388-073-9
- *Illinois Central Railroad 1854-1960 Photo Archive* ISBN 1-58388-063-1
- *Milwaukee Road 1850-1960 Photo Archive* ISBN 1-882256-61-1
- *Milwaukee Road Depots 1856-1954 Photo Archive* ISBN 1-58388-040-2
- *Show Trains of the 20th Century* ISBN 1-58388-030-5
- *Soo Line 1975-1992 Photo Archive* ISBN 1-882256-68-9
- *Steam Locomotives of the B&O Railroad Photo Archive* ISBN 1-58388-095-X
- *Streamliners to the Twin Cities Photo Archive 400, Twin Zephyrs & Hiawatha Trains* ISBN 1-58388-096-8
- *Trains of the Twin Ports Photo Archive, Duluth-Superior in the 1950s* ISBN 1-58388-003-8
- *Trains of the Circus 1872-1956* ISBN 1-58388-024-0
- *Trains of the Upper Midwest Photo Archive Steam & Diesel in the 1950s & 1960s* ISBN 1-58388-036-4
- *Wisconsin Central Limited 1987-1996 Photo Archive* ISBN 1-882256-75-1
- *Wisconsin Central Railway 1871-1909 Photo Archive* ISBN 1-882256-78-6

RECREATIONAL VEHICLES

- *Ski-Doo Racing Sleds 1960-2003 Photo Archive* ISBN 1-58388-105-0

TRUCKS

- *Autocar Trucks 1950-1987 Photo Archive* ISBN 1-58388-072-0
- *Beverage Trucks 1910-1975 Photo Archive* ISBN 1-882256-60-3
- *Brockway Trucks 1948-1961 Photo Archive** ISBN 1-882256-55-7
- *Chevrolet El Camino Photo History Incl. GMC Sprint & Caballero* ISBN 1-58388-044-5
- *Circus and Carnival Trucks 1923-2000 Photo Archive* ISBN 1-58388-048-8
- *Dodge B-Series Trucks Restorer's & Collector's Reference Guide and History* ISBN 1-58388-087-9
- *Dodge Pickups 1939-1978 Photo Album* ISBN 1-882256-82-4
- *Dodge Power Wagons 1940-1980 Photo Archive* ISBN 1-882256-89-1
- *Dodge Power Wagon Photo History* ISBN 1-58388-019-4
- *Dodge Ram Trucks 1994-2001 Photo History* ISBN 1-58388-051-8
- *Dodge Trucks 1929-1947 Photo Archive* ISBN 1-882256-36-0
- *Dodge Trucks 1948-1960 Photo Archive* ISBN 1-882256-37-9
- *Ford 4x4s 1935-1990 Photo History* ISBN 1-58388-079-8
- *Ford Heavy-Duty Trucks 1948-1998 Photo History* ISBN 1-58388-043-7
- *Freightliner Trucks 1937-1981 Photo Archive* ISBN 1-58388-090-9
- *Jeep 1941-2000 Photo Archive* ISBN 1-58388-021-6
- *Jeep Prototypes & Concept Vehicles Photo Archive* ISBN 1-58388-033-X
- *Mack Model AB Photo Archive** ISBN 1-882256-18-2
- *Mack AP Super-Duty Trucks 1926-1938 Photo Archive** ISBN 1-882256-54-9
- *Mack Model B 1953-1966 Volume 2 Photo Archive** ISBN 1-882256-34-4
- *Mack EB-EC-ED-EE-EF-EG-DE 1936-1951 Photo Archive** ISBN 1-882256-29-8
- *Mack EH-EJ-EM-EQ-ER-ES 1936-1950 Photo Archive** ISBN 1-882256-39-5
- *Mack FC-FCSW-NW 1936-1947 Photo Archive** ISBN 1-882256-28-X
- *Mack FG-FH-FJ-FK-FN-FP-FT-FW 1937-1950 Photo Archive** ISBN 1-882256-35-2
- *Mack LF-LH-LJ-LM-LT 1940-1956 Photo Archive** ISBN 1-882256-38-7
- *Mack Trucks Photo Gallery** ISBN 1-882256-88-3
- *New Car Carriers 1910-1998 Photo Album* ISBN 1-882256-98-0
- *Plymouth Commercial Vehicles Photo Archive* ISBN 1-58388-004-6
- *Refuse Trucks Photo Archive* ISBN 1-58388-042-9
- *RVs & Campers 1900-2000: An Illustrated History* ISBN 1-58388-064-X
- *Studebaker Trucks 1927-1940 Photo Archive* ISBN 1-882256-40-9
- *White Trucks 1900-1937 Photo Archive* ISBN 1-882256-80-8

TRACTORS & CONSTRUCTION EQUIPMENT

- *Case Tractors 1912-1959 Photo Archive* ISBN 1-882256-32-8
- *Caterpillar Photo Gallery* ISBN 1-882256-70-0
- *Caterpillar Pocket Guide The Track-Type Tractors 1925-1957* ISBN 1-58388-022-4
- *Caterpillar D-2 & R-2 Photo Archive* ISBN 1-882256-99-9
- *Caterpillar D-8 1933-1974 Photo Archive Incl. Diesel 75 & RD-8* ISBN 1-882256-96-4
- *Caterpillar Military Tractors Volume 1 Photo Archive* ISBN 1-882256-16-6
- *Caterpillar Military Tractors Volume 2 Photo Archive* ISBN 1-882256-17-4
- *Caterpillar Sixty Photo Archive* ISBN 1-882256-05-0
- *Caterpillar Ten Photo Archive Incl. 7c Fifteen & High Fifteen* ISBN 1-58388-011-9
- *Caterpillar Thirty Photo Archive 2ND Ed. Incl. Best Thirty, 6G Thirty & R-4* ISBN 1-58388-006-2
- *Circus & Carnival Tractors 1930-2001 Photo Archive* ISBN 1-58388-076-3
- *Cletrac and Oliver Crawlers Photo Archive* ISBN 1-882256-43-3
- *Classic American Steamrollers 1871-1935 Photo Archive* ISBN 1-58388-038-0
- *Farmall Cub Photo Archive* ISBN 1-882256-71-9
- *Farmall F-Series Photo Archive* ISBN 1-882256-02-6
- *Farmall Model H Photo Archive* ISBN 1-882256-03-4
- *Farmall Model M Photo Archive* ISBN 1-882256-15-8
- *Farmall Regular Photo Archive* ISBN 1-882256-14-X
- *Farmall Super Series Photo Archive* ISBN 1-882256-49-2
- *Fordson 1917-1928 Photo Archive* ISBN 1-882256-33-6
- *Hart-Parr Photo Archive* ISBN 1-882256-08-5
- *Holt Tractors Photo Archive* ISBN 1-882256-10-7
- *International TracTracTor Photo Archive* ISBN 1-882256-48-4
- *John Deere Model A Photo Archive* ISBN 1-882256-12-3
- *John Deere Model D Photo Archive* ISBN 1-882256-00-X
- *Marion Construction Machinery 1884-1975 Photo Archive* ISBN 1-58388-060-7
- *Marion Mining & Dredging Machines Photo Archive* ISBN 1-58388-088-7
- *Oliver Tractors Photo Archive* ISBN 1-882256-09-3
- *Russell Graders Photo Archive* ISBN 1-882256-11-5
- *Twin City Tractor Photo Archive* ISBN 1-882256-06-9

CLASSIC SEAGRAVE
1935 - 1951 PHOTO ARCHIVE

Walt McCall & Matt Lee

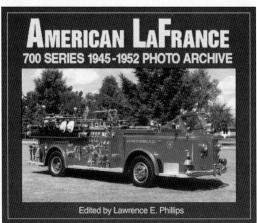

AMERICAN LaFrance
700 SERIES 1945-1952 PHOTO ARCHIVE

Edited by Lawrence E. Phillips

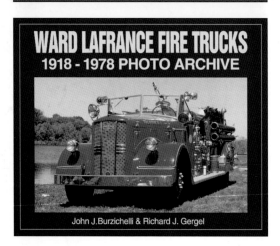

WARD LAFRANCE FIRE TRUCKS
1918 - 1978 PHOTO ARCHIVE

John J. Burzichelli & Richard J. Gergel

More great books from
Iconografix

Classic Seagrave 1935-1951 Photo Archive
ISBN 1-58388-034-8

Pirsch Fire Apparatus 1890-1991 Photo Archive
ISBN 1-58388-082-8

**American LaFrance 700 Series 1945-1952
Photo Archive** ISBN 1-882256-090-5

Young Fire Equipment 1932-1991 Photo Archive
ISBN 1-58388-015-1

Ward LaFrance 1918-1978 Photo Archive
ISBN 1-58388-013-5

Crown Firecoach 1951-1985 Photo Archive
ISBN 1-58388-047-X

Maxim Fire Apparatus 1914-1989 Photo Archive
ISBN 1-58388-050-X

Iconografix, Inc.
P.O. Box 446, Dept BK,
Hudson, WI 54016
For a **free catalog** call: 1-800-289-3504

CROWN FIRECOACH
1951 - 1985 PHOTO ARCHIVE

Chuck Madderom

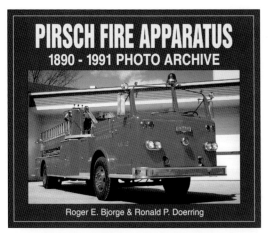

PIRSCH FIRE APPARATUS
1890 - 1991 PHOTO ARCHIVE

Roger E. Bjorge & Ronald P. Doerring

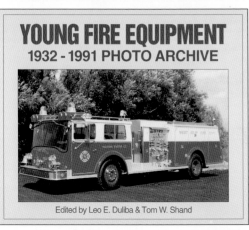

YOUNG FIRE EQUIPMENT
1932 - 1991 PHOTO ARCHIVE

Edited by Leo E. Duliba & Tom W. Shand

MAXIM FIRE APPARATUS
1914 - 1989 PHOTO ARCHIVE

Howard T. Smith